GW00645424

# Birds
## *of* Lepe

**with illustrations by Chris Button and photographs by the author.**

*Cover photograph, design and typesetting by Mike Creighton.*

*Published by Chalkhill Publishing.*

*ISBN 978-0-9931118-3-9*

*With thanks to the 'Friends of Lepe' and to the local County Councillor, Alexis McEvoy, for their support.*

*For Maps, base map and data from OpenStreetMap and OpenStreetMap Foundation.*

*Printed by PrintDomain.*

*20 years of wings over the water at Lepe, Hampshire*

**Philip Fawkes**

# Birds
## *of* Lepe
# 2000–2020

**It is not intended that this account be scientific or exhaustive. Its purpose is to provide a relatively broad and hopefully informative account of the birds seen at Lepe over two decades, with specific reference to the past five years.** It is aimed as much at the casual observer as it is the more experienced, with brief guidance given on what species may be observed where, in what period of the year, and in what numbers.

For each species, there is an introductory paragraph in which its present-day status at Lepe is summarised and, in some cases, put into a county or national context.

The second paragraph, and subsequent paragraphs where applicable, present an historical record of each species during the period 2000–2020. This is generally in the form of a summary, but where there are fewer than fifteen records for the twenty-year period, all sightings are documented. References to records before 2000 are written in italics, as are the names, in parentheses, of those who submitted records of species uncommon to Lepe.

Species categories comply with the BOU maintained British List (9th edition, revised June 2021).

Sightings of rare species to the County have only been included if they have been accepted by the Rarities Panel of the Hampshire Ornithological Society and, where applicable, by the British Birds Rarities Committee (BBRC).

## Species Recorded

During the twenty-year period, 206 full species were recorded at Lepe, with an additional three sub-species (Pale-bellied Brent Goose, Black Brant, and White Wagtail) included in the subsequent Check List.

This tally may not compare too favourably with those of other coastal locations in Hampshire, most notably Lymington Marshes, Titchfield Haven, and Farlington Marshes, but given the relatively low level of observer coverage and limited range of habitat, this number is impressive and includes several migrant/vagrant species classified as 'rare', either to Hampshire or to the British Isles.

Many of the records in the first decade of the period were contributed by Jeff Ross, who spent endless hours walking the Lepe Loop. I am grateful to him for his contributions, and I acknowledge and thank all those who have submitted their records through Going Birding, BirdGuides, The Lepe Bird Group, and other local and not so local sources.

I am also indebted to Chris Button for allowing me to use some of his sketches of species I have seen over the years.

## Recording Area (See Map 1)

Lepe Country Park is located on the south eastern edge of the New Forest National Park.

It encompasses approximately a mile of the Solent's coastline, being primarily a beach location, but the park also stretches inland for a distance of between 10m and 500m.

The habitats that are found here include: grassland, wildflower meadows, scrub, mixed deciduous woodland, stands of mixed pine, hedgerows, coastal fringe plants, sand dunes, shingle beach and spit, lagoons, wetland areas, and reed beds. Being a country park there is a mixture of managed areas for recreation and education as well as those managed more for conservation.

Site designations include: Site of Special Scientific Interest (SSSI), Site of Importance for Nature Conservation (SINC), National Nature Reserve (NNR), Local Nature Reserve (LNR), and Wetlands of International Importance (Ramsar).

The site is a haven for wildlife all year round. It is nationally important for migratory birds (e.g. Brent Geese). The Solent, which the park borders, has a large expanse of Eel Grass and many species of seaweed.

The terrestrial habitats are generally well looked after and in good condition and provide habitats for a wide range of wildlife.

Although the Lepe Country Park marketing material refers to the five-mile 'Lepe Loop', most of the hours spent in the field tended to be within easy walking distance of the café and included the coastal path west to Inchmery (1) and east to Stone Point (2) and Stansore Pools (3) – and beyond to the D-Day Monument (4) and the private beach of the Cadland Estate (5).

There are references in this Report to the Nature Reserve (6), where there is a public hide which looks out onto the lower reaches of the Dark Water Estuary and the 'boardwalk' which is an attractive habitat for passerines.

Specific sites along the marked route of the 'Lepe Loop', which is to the west of the Dark Water Estuary and is frequently cited in the species' texts, include Coastguard Cottages (7), East Hill Copse (8), East Hill Farm (9) and, following a two-mile walk over farmland and through woods, Exbury Road near Inchmery (Three Stones) (10), from where the circular loop is completed by walking east back to the Coastguard Cottages.

The recording area is punctuated by habitats that are private and inaccessible. These include the grounds of Inchmery House (11) and Lepe House (12) to the west of the café, whilst to the east one might only speculate as to what may be found in scrub along the tarmacadam road from Stansore Point to Stone Farm (13) or in the mixed woodland behind Stansore Pools, known as Allwood Copse, that is on the Cadland Estate.

There are points from which to view the Dark Water Estuary which in many ways is the epicentre of Lepe. These include the road bridge, the hide, and the top field behind Coastguard Cottages. Access otherwise is limited and given the terrain, not advisable anyway.

## The Future (See Map 2)

It is hoped that a more thorough bird breeding survey will be undertaken over the next three to five years to include all accessible wetland areas, particularly along the Dark Water Estuary, and the wooded enclosures of Grassy Copse (1), East Hill Copse (2), The Moor (3), Cump Copse (4), and Little Haxland Copse (5), where there are designated footpaths.

It is anticipated that more hours spent watching the sea during spring and autumn would reveal the true extent of seabird passage through the Solent, whilst watching and listening during the first two hours of light in September and October at Stone Point would improve our knowledge of passerine movement past Lepe.

There is still much to learn!

Philip Fawkes

August 2021

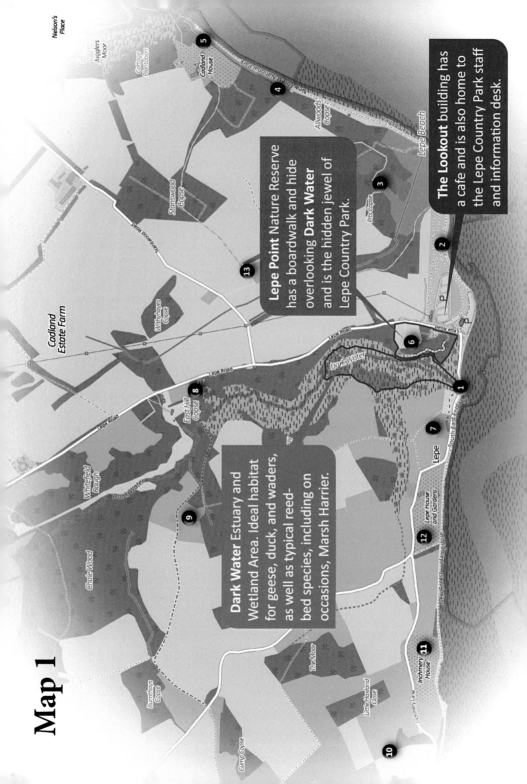

# Map 1

**The Lookout** building has a cafe and is also home to the Lepe Country Park staff and information desk.

**Lepe Point** Nature Reserve has a boardwalk and hide overlooking **Dark Water** and is the hidden jewel of Lepe Country Park.

**Dark Water** Estuary and Wetland Area. Ideal habitat for geese, duck, and waders, as well as typical reed-bed species, including on occasions, Marsh Harrier.

Nelson's Place

Jugglers Moor

Cottage Plantation

Cadland House

New Forest National Park

Allwoods Copse

Lepe Beach

Hartsgrove

Pits Copse

Stanswood Copse

Stanswood Road

Withyhayes Copse

Cadland Estate Farm

Lepe Road

Dark Water

Lepe Road

Lepe Road

East Hill Copse

Whitefield Rough

Dark Water

Chale Wood

Lepe

South East Hangar

Lepe House and Gardens

New Forest - Hampshire

Burnham's Copse

The Moor

Little Howland Close

Inchmery House

Inchmery Lane

Camp Copse

# Map 2

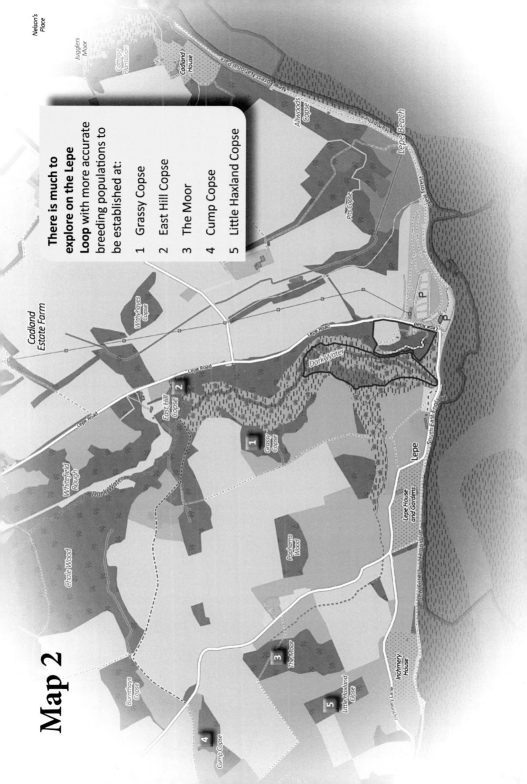

**There is much to explore on the Lepe Loop** with more accurate breeding populations to be established at:

1 Grassy Copse
2 East Hill Copse
3 The Moor
4 Cump Copse
5 Little Haxland Copse

## THE CHECK-LISTS

The check-lists follow the British Ornithological Union systematic order using the common names.

A full list of the species recorded giving both the common and scientific name is shown in the appendix to this report.

### Dark-bellied Brent Goose

**Current Status:** A winter visitor frequenting the foreshore between Stansore Point and the Coastguard Cottages. Numbers build from late September, but the highest counts are mostly post-New Year. The typical diurnal pattern is for birds to land and feed on the ebb and flow of the tide, seeming to prefer spending the high water on the Beaulieu River and the low water at sites to the east.

**Summary of Records:** The highest count for the twenty-year period was 620 on 6th Mar 2015, feeding mid-tide between the café and Coastguard Cottages. Interestingly, not one was present there at high tide.

See Table 1 for annual maximum counts for the period 2000–2020.

The earliest winter return date was 10th September (2015). Most winters, the population declined in April, with most having gone by early May, although there was an exceptional count of 560 on 8th May 2000. In only five of the twenty years from 2000 were there June–August records, the last in 2007 (1, 8th June).

### Pale-bellied Brent Goose

**Current Status:** This is still regarded as a sub-species of the Brant Goose, the others being Dark-bellied Brent Goose and Black Brant. It is not common in Hampshire. Most Lepe records refer to individuals with Dark-bellied Brent Goose, either feeding along the foreshore between the café and the road bridge or flying to the Beaulieu River on the incoming tide.

**All Records 2000–2020** (7): There was a first-winter bird on 1st Mar and 24th Apr 2001 (*RB Wynn*), but no other record until 11th Apr 2009 (*PD Winter*), and a further five years (2014) before one was seen on

Pale-bellied Brent Goose (centre foreground) with Dark-bellied

several dates, again in April, and with Dark-bellied Brent feeding along the foreshore between the café and road bridge.

In 2015, there were records of an individual on several dates between January and April, and again in the early winter of that year, with two off Stansore Point on 3rd December.

A pair was present from 15th to 22nd Apr 2016, which the observer, Bob Chapman, thought might have been Canadian birds that had wintered in France and were heading back.

There was a single record in 2017 (10th February) and several through January–March in 2018, which presumably referred to the same individual.

## Black Brant

**All Records 2000–2020** (1): A single record of a bird on the foreshore in front of the café with Dark-bellied Brent Geese on 12th Nov 2011 (*PD Jones*).

## Red-breasted Goose

**All Records 2000–2020** (1): An adult with Dark-bellied Brent Geese on 24th–25th Sept 2000 (*JG Ross, D Taylor, DJ Unsworth*).

## Canada Goose

**Current Status:** Resident but rarely in numbers exceeding ten and usually confined to the upper reaches of the Dark Water Estuary and to Stansore Pools, where breeding takes place.

**Summary of Records:** Counts of 72 on 20th Feb 2006 and 27 on 14th August the same year were exceptional. One or two pairs have regularly bred at Stansore and/or the Dark Water Estuary, with four pairs in 2015, the maximum in any one year.

## Barnacle Goose

**All Records 2000–2020** (4): One present on 8th May 2000 (*JG Ross*) and a group of 11 grazing in the fields behind Coastguard Cottages on 3rd Mar 2006 (*JG Ross*). A single individual consorted with Brent Geese between 2nd and 11th Jan 2014 (*PE Jones & A Lester*) and three flew east past Stansore Point on 3rd Nov 2016 (*PF Fawkes*).

## Greylag Goose

**Current Status:** With the increase in numbers along the west bank of the Beaulieu River, often visible from the road bridge, further occurrences at Lepe are anticipated, as is breeding.

**Summary of Records:** The two highest counts on the Dark Water Estuary were 105 on 25th Sept 2000 and 65 on 3rd Aug 2004, since when there have only been five records, including a party of 62 on 17th Aug 2018. The first breeding pair, raising three young, was recorded in 2020 on the upper reaches of the Dark Water Estuary.

## European White-fronted Goose

**All Records 2000–2020** (1): A first-year individual on the foreshore with Dark-bellied Brent Geese on 13th Oct 2016 (*PF Fawkes*) was presumably the same individual seen on the Lower Test Marshes the following day.

## Greenland White-fronted Goose

**All Records 2000–2020** (1):
An individual with Dark-bellied Brent Geese off Stansore Point from 8th to 15th Nov 2000 was the second record of 'Greenland' White-fronted Goose for Hampshire (*JG Ross, D Taylor*).

## Mute Swan

**Current Status:** Present all year, with breeding pair(s) likely on the Dark Water and/or Stansore Pools, and winter records from the Solent.

**Summary of Records:** There were no winter gatherings of note, but at least one breeding pair was successful from 2015, nesting on Stansore Pools and/or the Dark Water Estuary.

## Egyptian Goose

**Current Status:** A recent increase in the feral population from west of the Beaulieu River may cross over and be seen more frequently either flying along the coast or settled on the upper reaches of the Dark Water Estuary.

**All Records 2000–2020** (3): The first record at Lepe was in 2017, when two flew west past Stone Point on 15th June. Seven flew east from the mouth of the Beaulieu River on 12th Jan 2018 and four were on the Dark Water on 31st May 2020, with two still present there on 10th June.

## Shelduck

**Current Status:** Present in small numbers, typically low single figures, on the Dark Water Estuary or on Stansore Pools. Breeding pairs on Badminston Common may be seen bringing their brood down to the coast in July/August.

**Summary of Records:** Exceptionally high counts were 27 on 5th Jan 2008, 25 on 10th Jan 2010, 24 on 4th May 2014, and 20 on 28th Mar 2019.

Breeding at Lepe was confirmed in 2000 when a pair reared seven young on the Dark Water and suspected there in 2014 when chicks were seen with the parents striking out into the Solent, although these could have come down from Badminston Common. Breeding was confirmed on the Dark Water Estuary in 2020.

## Mandarin

**Current Status:** There is a lack of coverage where habitat is most suitable, which is in the upper reaches of the Dark Water Estuary to the east of East Hill Farm.

**Summary of Records:** Breeding was confirmed in each of the years 2001 to 2005, with two pairs in 2002. There have been no records since a pair was present at East Hill Copse on 15th Jan 2017.

## Garganey

*Pre-2000:* *A drake flew east on 10th May 1993 (RA Chapman).*

**All Records 2000–2020** (1): A report of two on 15th Sept 2013 (*observer(s) unknown*) was unsubstantiated, but there was a confirmed sighting of an immature male on Stansore Pools on 23rd Feb 2020 (*RA Chapman*).

## Shoveler

**Current Status:** An irregular winter visitor (October–February) on the Dark Water and very occasionally at Stansore. Small numbers may be seen at the mouth of the Beaulieu River, best viewed from west of Lepe House.

**Summary of Records:** The latest departure date at the end of winter was 15th April (2006) and the first return date was 7th September (2018). Most records were in the period November to January, with double-figure counts on the Dark Water Estuary of 15 on 10th Jan 2009, ten on 9th Jan 2010, ten on 30th Dec 2015, and the highest number, 26 on 17th Nov 2017. In addition to two records on Stansore Pools, three were on the Solent off Stone Point on 28th Oct 2018.

## Gadwall

**Current Status:** Present in the winter months on the Dark Water and generally visible from the road bridge or the hide.

**Summary of Records:** Although there were several years with no sightings posted, it was recorded annually from 2013. Other than 28 on 10th Jan 2010, numbers were in single figures until post-2014, when there were double-figure counts in Dec 2015 (day-maximum, 24 on 12th); Dec 2018 (day-maximum, 40 on 11th); Jan 2019 (day-maximum, 18 on 2nd); and Feb 2020 (day-maximum, 20 on 25th).

Although two pairs were present on Stansore Pools throughout May 2011 and on the Dark Water during May/June 2015, and three pairs were recorded at Lepe on 2nd May 2018, breeding was not confirmed at any of the sites.

## Wigeon

**Current Status:** A winter visitor, present between late August and March, but not regular. Winter rafts on the Solent off Needs Ore, barely visible from Lepe, may occasionally be seen flying into the Dark Water Estuary or, more rarely, onto Stansore Pools.

**Summary of Records:** The latest date for spring departure was 24th March (2012) and the earliest winter return was 27th August (2014). The highest counts on the Dark Water were in 2013, when numbers increased from 173 on 17th November to 380 on 4th December.

Otherwise, the only counts exceeding 50 were on 19th Oct 2002 (80); 6th Dec 2003 (80); 21st Dec 2005 (73); 28th Dec 2014 (70); 19th Dec 2015 (65); and 1st Jan 2016 (60).

## Mallard

**Current Status:** Present in the winter months, but rarely in numbers exceeding 20. A small group of non-breeding males may be seen on the upper reaches of the Dark Water.

**Summary of Records:** A paucity of records. The only double-figure counts were 50 on 28th Oct 2001, 75 on 25th Dec 2004, and 42 on 1st July 2009, which was an exceptionally high number for this time of the year.

## Pintail

**Current Status:** Scarce winter visitor, but may be present to the east of Inchmery House, where winter numbers at the mouth to the Beaulieu River may typically reach 20 or more.

**Summary of Records:** The latest spring departure date was 20th March (2005), when 30 flew east through the Solent, whilst the earliest date for winter return was 7th September (2018).

Most records came from the Dark Water Estuary, but no count there exceeded 19 (Feb 2013), whilst a day-maximum of 40 was at the mouth of the Beaulieu River on 5th Jan 2020.

## Teal

**Current Status:** A winter visitor (August to April) that may be seen regularly in small numbers on the Dark Water (from the road bridge) and on Stansore Pools, but rarely on the Solent, except for occasional rafts off Gull Island, Needs Ore.

**Summary of Records:** The annual maxima in Table 1 combine the two principal sites of the Dark Water and Stansore Pools and relate to the months October–March.

There were very few records for the period May–July. Flocks of up to 50 were recorded alighting from a private and inaccessible pond on the Cadland Estate to occasionally settle on Stansore Pools.

## Tufted Duck

**Current Status:** A common winter visitor in Hampshire to rivers and freshwater pools. Neither the Dark Water nor Stansore Pools are suitable habitat, but there is a likely presence on the small freshwater reservoir on the Cadland Estate, but where there is no public access.

**All Records 2000–2020** (6): With the exception of one on 11th Sept 2004, all records were in late spring/summer, with four on the Dark Water on 26th May 2010; two at Stansore on 20th May 2012; four (3m, 1f) off Stansore Point on 29th Apr 2014; two pairs on the Dark Water on 23rd May 2015; and a female briefly on the Dark Water before flying to Needs Ore on 7th June 2020.

## Scaup

***Pre-2000:*** *A single individual on 13th Jan 1997 (J Keddie).*

**All Records 2000–2020** (1): A male seemingly flew in a circle, from Calshot Spit to Stansore Point and back, on 21st Jan 2017 (*PF Fawkes*).

## Eider

**Current Status:** May occasionally be seen flying east or west mid-channel between regular winter rafts off Hill Head and Lymington–Sowley. Sightings of individuals in winter on the water off Lepe are not uncommon.

A drake Eider
Solent from Coastguard Cottages, May 2017

**Summary of Records:** Recorded in every year, except 2011, when there was poor coverage. Records were exclusive to the Solent, either on the water, or more often flying east or west past Stansore Point. Most records were between late October and mid-March, although there were summer sightings, presumably of non-breeding birds from further west along the Solent, which included one on 19th July 2002, nine on 22nd June 2003, six on 31st May 2004, 20 on 29th May 2005, and four on 18th May 2017.

The maximum winter count was 180 offshore on 14th Apr 2006 (*A Lewis*). The only other counts to exceed 50 were 80 on 23rd Dec 2006 and 51 on 31st Mar 2007. See Table 1 for annual maxima.

## Velvet Scoter

***Pre-2000:*** *A male on 8th Feb 1994 (P Matthews).*

**All Records 2000–2020** (3): One flew west through the Solent on 28th Apr 2001 (*NJ Hull*); four (2m 1f) flew east on 28th Oct 2012 (*G Horacek-Davis*); and one was off Gull Island, west of the Coastguard Cottages, on 16th Nov 2013 (*observer unknown*).

## Common Scoter

**Current Status:** Stragglers may be seen flying east or west through the Solent irrespective of the time of year. Mostly seen in winter, but not uncommon in summer. Spring and autumn passage through the Solent past Lepe is limited.

**Summary of Records:** There were no records for 2003 or for the years between 2007 and 2012, the latter possibly because of lack of coverage. Most records were of small groups flying through the Solent in the winter months, the dates of the three highest counts (80, Nov 2000; 80, Jan 2014; and 40, Feb 2013) suggesting that birds did not pass through the Solent in any significant number during spring and autumn migration. A party of 17 flying east on 8th Apr 2018 were likely passage birds.

There were examples of long-staying individuals, as was the case in 2018, when a female was seen off the café from 9th January to 10th February.

## Long-tailed Duck

**Current Status:** An uncommon winter visitor to the Solent and to Hampshire generally.

**All Records 2000–2020** (2):
A relatively long-staying female was seen regularly from 13th Nov 2003 to 3rd Mar 2004 (*JG Ross et al.*).

A female, present from 28th Nov 2013, was joined by a drake on 6th December (*MC Adams, PD Winter*) and the pair was recorded almost daily on the Solent between Coastguard Cottages and Inchmery House (at the mouth of the Beaulieu River) until 16th Feb 2014, after which the male was seen irregularly up to 21st March.

## Goldeneye

**All Records 2000–2020** (1): A female landed on the Solent west of the road bridge on 31st Oct 2019 (*R Chapman*).

## Goosander:

*Pre-2000: A single record of a female on 29th Nov 1995 (G Horacek-Davis)*

**All Records 2000–2020** (3): A female/immature flew east through the Solent on 26th Oct 2012 (*NR Jones*), three (2f, 1m) flew west past Stansore Point on 3rd Dec 2015 (*PF Fawkes*),

and a female was close inshore near the café on 8th Dec 2020 (*P James*).

## Red-breasted Merganser:

**Current Status:** One or two may occasionally be seen on the Solent, anywhere between Stansore Point and the mouth of the Beaulieu River, during the winter months.

**Summary of Records:** Recorded every year, but rarely more than half a dozen sightings for each, and almost exclusively between October (earliest on 30th, 2004) and April (latest on 21st, 2005).

Five east through the Solent on 8th Sept 2015 was the only record outside of these months. The highest single count was 15 on 7th Nov 2004. See Table 1 for annual maxima.

## Red-legged Partridge

**Current Status:** A pen-released species, rather than feral, with numbers highest in autumn and most frequently seen in small groups in the fields to the east of the café and around Stansore Pools (Cadland Estate) or along Exbury Road by Lepe Farm.

**Summary of Records:** As expected, given its status as an estate-reared species, the highest covey numbers were in the late summer and early autumn. Triple-figure counts included 110 on 26th Aug 2003, 100 on 15th Sept 2005, and 120 (to the north and east of the campsite) on 9th Sept 2020.

## Grey Partridge

**All Records 2000–2020** (1): Eight on the Cadland Estate behind Stansore Marshes on 19th Oct 2009 would have been pen-released and not feral.

## Pheasant

**Current Status:** Present all year, with a small breeding population, typically five–ten pairs, outside of the Exbury and Cadland Estates.

**Summary of Records:** The highest count was 21 on 29th Apr 2011. Otherwise, pairs were recorded only on Stansore Pools and the upper reaches of the Dark Water Estuary.

## Nightjar

**All Records 2000–2020** (1): One was flushed from cover along the boardwalk on the Reserve in daylight hours on 29th Aug 2010 (*JG Ross*).

## Swift

**Current Status:** A summer migrant which is not always conspicuous at Lepe and which is unlikely to be seen after August.

**Summary of Records:** The earliest arrival date was 28th April (2006). Most records were in May, including the day-maximum of 16 flying north across the Solent and over Stansore Point on 2nd (2014). The last date in autumn was 28th August (2020).

## Cuckoo

**Current Status:** An irregular summer visitor that may be seen, or heard, on the Dark Water Estuary from mid-April and into May.

**Summary of Records:** Recorded in ten of the twenty years. The earliest arrival date was 11th April (2001), whilst the only record outside of April–May was on 2nd July 2000.

## Stock Dove

**Current Status:** A relatively common resident which is almost exclusive to the woods and fields at Lepe Farm and East Hill Farm.

Stock Dove
East Hill, December 2019

**Summary of Records:** A flock of 50 feeding in fields inland from the Dark Water Estuary in Oct 2003 and 2004 was indicative of autumn passage. There were few records submitted, otherwise.

## Wood Pigeon

**Current Status:** Abundant, particularly during autumn when large passage movements may be seen at the coast. Whilst most common in the woods and fields at Lepe Farm and East Hill Farm, it is widespread across the recording area, including in the immediate vicinity of the café, with an estimated breeding population overall in the range of 20–40 pairs.

**Summary of Records:** There were few counts recorded and coverage was generally poor. There was evidence of breeding in suitable habitat inland around the farms, but no records to prove such.

## Turtle Dove

**Current Status:** A scarce summer visitor and passage migrant with the British and Hampshire breeding population having seriously declined in the past forty years.

**All Records 2000–2020** (8):
*All records submitted by Jeff Ross unless otherwise specified.* There were three spring records: two on 15th May 2005 and singles on 13th May 2008 (*AS Rhodes*) and 27th May 2012 (*PD Jones*). Although individuals were present on 20th June 2004, 20th July 2004, and 25th June 2005, breeding in the recording area was not suspected during the twenty-year period. The two autumn records were of singles on 2nd Aug 2001 and 4th Sept 2008 (*SA Woolfries*).

## Collared Dove

**Current Status:** One or two pairs are regularly around the café, at Lepe Farm and at East Hill Farm. The breeding population is estimated at between two and six pairs.

**Summary of Records:** A flock of 23 on 20th Oct 2003 was the only significant record and there were no references to breeding numbers.

## Water Rail

**Current Status:** Resident and regularly seen, or more often heard, on the Dark Water (around the hide, along the boardwalk and in the reeds in the valley behind the Coastguard Cottages) and on Stansore Pools.

Both the winter and breeding populations are difficult to gauge owing to their skulking behaviour but based on calls it is estimated that between three and five territories may be held each summer.

**Summary of Records:** There were records of one or two for all the years (2000–2020) and covering every month over that period, except for June. Breeding was confirmed in 2003 when an adult and two young were seen on 15th July. There were four calling on the Dark Water on 19th Nov 2020, the most recorded on one day.

## Moorhen

**Current Status:** Regularly present at Stansore (along the channel that runs to the Point), and on the Dark Water, but probably under-reported and more information is required on its current winter and breeding status.

**Summary of Records:** The highest count was 21 on 14th Aug 2001 and the only confirmed breeding was in 2011.

## Coot

**Current Status:** The small breeding population on the Dark Water Estuary from 2014 to 2018 is no longer evident, but there is likely to be a small winter population on the reservoir (private site on Cadland Estate) behind Stansore Pools.

**Summary of Records:** The first 'official' record at Lepe was on the Dark Water on 5th May 2013 and was described by Jeff Ross as "unusual here". This was followed by two April records, in 2014 and 2017, which heralded an unprecedented increase in its presence on the Dark Water during the winter of 2017/18. Three pairs bred in 2018, and although young were seen being taken by the resident pair of Marsh Harrier, there were still 12 on the Dark Water in December. There were no sightings there in 2020.

## Little Grebe

**Current Status:** Present in winter, but although no evidence of breeding, there is suitable habitat higher up the Dark Water Estuary. Rarely seen on the sea, except occasionally at the mouth of the Beaulieu River (1–3), when viewable from east of Inchmery.

**Summary of Records:**
The latest spring departure date was 29th March (2019), and the earliest winter return was 4th September (2006 and 2015). The highest counts were nine on 6th Dec 2008 and eight on 14th Nov 2013.

## Red-necked Grebe

**Current Status:** A very scarce winter visitor and passage migrant to the south coast and particularly rare in the west Solent.

***Pre-2000:** (3): Singles on 12th Jan 1986, 13th and 19th Feb 1987, and 8–9th Feb 1994.*

**All Records 2000–2020** (1): The record of one on 8th Mar 2005 (BirdGuides) was accepted by HOS Rarities Committee, but there was no information given as to where on the Solent, or whether on the water or in flight.

## Great Crested Grebe

**Current Status:** A regular winter visitor, exclusive to the open sea (October to April), with the highest congregation normally between the mouth of the Beaulieu River and Coastguard Cottages.

**Summary of Records:** Although the day-maximum for most years reached double figures, a count of 57 on 10th Jan 2009 was exceptional off Lepe. Numbers were much lower post-2016, which was in sharp contrast to winter gatherings in the Southampton Water. There were two summer records – a single individual on 9th June 2018 and six to the east of Inchmery on 3rd May 2019. Table 1 shows winter maxima 2000–2020.

## Slavonian Grebe

**Current Status:** A potential winter visitor (November–March) on the Solent, most commonly at west Lepe, but there have been fewer post-2016 records.

**Summary of Records:** The two records from east Lepe off Stansore Point were on 7th Dec 2010 (2) and 30th Jan 2016 (3). Most sightings were at the mouth to the Beaulieu River, where the highest count in the twenty-year period was seven on 16th Feb 2014. The last record was on 20th Jan 2018.

## Black-necked Grebe

**Current Status:** An irregular winter visitor, most likely to be seen near the mouth of the Beaulieu River.

**Summary of Records:** One to three recorded (November–March) every calendar year except for 2011, 2016, and 2019, and almost exclusively to the west of Coastguard Cottages at the mouth of the Beaulieu River. The earliest winter return was 1st November (2003) and the latest spring departure date, 27th March (2001).

Highest counts were six during the winter of 2002/03 (5th Jan 2003); seven in 2003/04 (24th Mar 2004); seven in 2004/05 (5th Dec 2004); and six in 2005/06 (11th Jan 2006). There were only three records following the

late winter of 2013/14, which were of one or two between 9th Jan and 15th Feb 2015, from 15th Jan to 5th Feb 2017, and on 8th Jan 2018.

## Oystercatcher

**Current Status:** Present daily throughout the winter when feeding on the foreshore between the café and the sluice gate or flying to and from the mouth of the Beaulieu River (Gull Island) on the rising tide.

**Summary of Records:**  Whilst the highest low-water counts were typically in spring or autumn, with 174 on 8th Sept 2002 being the day-maximum for the period 2000–2020, there were counts exceeding 50 in the summer months (May, June, and July) in all years between 2000 and 2006.

Numbers reached triple figures in Feb 2010, in Aug 2014 and 2015, and in Sept 2018.

Table 2 gives the annual maximum for those years in which records were submitted.

## Avocet

**Current Status:** Most likely to be seen in spring, either as a passage migrant or a wanderer from further along the coast at Needs Ore or Lymington, where there are breeding colonies.

**Summary of Records:** The first records were in 2010 when there were singletons on Stansore Pools on 10th–20th January and on 23rd December. Most records, thereafter, were in late winter to early spring, but not in every year.

The maximum count was eight on 29th Feb 2012, the year when there was evidence of spring passage, with four flying east through the Solent on 5th and 27th May, and six present on Stansore Pools on 2nd June.

A pair was regularly seen between 4th and 20th Apr 2013, but only a single individual was there through May and June. In 2019, a pair took up residence from 5th April to 5th May but there was no evidence of breeding.

There was only one autumn record, a single individual on Stansore Pools on 11th–13th Oct 2016.

## Lapwing

**Current Status:** Present on the Dark Water, or on adjacent fields to the east of Lepe Farm, from late July to late March, with mid-winter counts of 50–100 likely. There is suitable habitat on the Dark Water for a breeding pair(s), an event that is anticipated.

**Summary of Records:** There were triple-figure counts in five of the twenty winters, exclusively November/December, with a maximum of 250 on 26th Dec 2013. Breeding was confirmed on the Dark Water in 2000, but not proven thereafter, although 'prospecting' was evident in 2020. Table 2 gives winter maximum counts for years in which records were submitted.

## Golden Plover

**Current Status:** Rare at Lepe (first recorded in 2016) and yet present further west with a peak winter population at Lymington often exceeding 200.

All Records (4): The two records for 2016 came from Stansore Pools and were of single individuals on 24th February (*GJ Steaggles*) and 3rd November (*PF Fawkes*), whilst the two for 2018 were of a group of ten flying east along the coast on 3rd March (*R Chapman*) and of one, also flying east and calling persistently, on 4th October (*PF Fawkes*).

## Grey Plover

**Current Status:** A common winter visitor (September–April) seen regularly feeding along the foreshore between the road bridge and Stansore Point but in numbers rarely into double figures. Single birds occasionally present on Stansore Pools. High-water roosts may be seen at the mouth of the Beaulieu River (Inchmery) with the highest concentration in winter.

**Summary of Records:** Numbers tabulated in Table 2 refer to feeding and roosting counts at the mouth of the Beaulieu River. Here there were triple-figure counts in the period 2000–2020 in Sept 2002 (101), Dec 2003 (130), Jan 2005 (181), Feb 2017 (124), and Jan 2019 (140). There is no reason to assume that there were not high-water roosts for winters in which counts were not recorded.

May records, of which there were several over the twenty years, including 21 on 4th 2006 and 15 flying east on 4th 2017, were indicative of spring migration, whilst six in summer plumage on 1st Aug 2015 and 40 feeding at low water on 26th Aug 2003 were on autumn passage. There were no records for June/July.

## Ringed Plover

**Current Status:** Regular feeding parties may be seen between the sluice gate and the café, numbers depending on the state of the tide and the time of year. As the tide rises, so the majority either fly west to the Beaulieu River or east to the Cadland Estate foreshore where they enjoy little or no disturbance.

Ringed Plover
Stansore, April 2019

**Summary of Records:** With the exception of a high-tide roost of 50 on 19th Oct 2009, all counts given in Table 2 were taken at low tide. Given the presence of one–two pairs attempting, but rarely succeeding, to breed on the beach between the café and Stansore Point, or on the Stansore

Pools, there were records for all months of every year between 2000 and 2020.

In some years, there was a dearth of recorded counts, but where there was data, it showed a pattern of more marked autumn than spring passage, with a day-maximum of 180 on 14th Oct 2015. The highest winter number was 80 in Dec 2002, whilst breeding was confirmed in 2004, when a pair successfully reared one young.

## Little Ringed Plover

**Current Status:** An uncommon spring and autumn passage migrant which may be a candidate for breeding on the Dark Water Estuary in the future.

**All Records 2000–2020** (12): The first five records were on the Dark Water and seen by Jeff Ross. They were of single birds on 14th Apr 2001, 12th Apr 2004, 9th–12th Apr 2005, and 26th Aug 2005, and two on 8th June 2007.

There were singletons, again on the Dark Water, on 19th Mar 2009 (*MC Adams*) and 3rd–21st Apr 2013 (*PA Warne & JG Ross*), with two there on 5th May, but with no evidence of breeding.

There were single individuals on the Dark Water on 12th June 2015 (*SJ Jackson*) and 23rd Sept 2017 (*PF Fawkes*), and on Stansore Pools on 4th Aug 2018 and 1st Apr 2019 (*PF Fawkes*).

## Whimbrel

**Current Status:** A regular passage migrant with small groups often seen flying east through the Solent in April and May.

**Summary of Records:** There were records for most years, mostly in April and May when passage east through the Solent was observed. Significant periods of movement included 34 on 4th May 2003; a total of 128 on six dates between 3rd and 11th May 2004; 30 on 29th Apr 2014; 17 on 17th May 2015; and in 2019, 27 on 15th April in one hour and 16 on 30th April in half an hour.

Autumn records were few (four on the Dark Water on 28th July being an exception) and the only winter sighting was of an individual along the tideline on 10th Nov 2015.

## Curlew

**Current Status:** Absent in May (small New Forest breeding population) but present in winter and most numerous in late summer/autumn when on passage. High-water roosts may be witnessed in the field behind the Coastguard Cottages: otherwise seen feeding along the tideline at low water.

**Summary of Records:** The annual maxima for years where numbers were in double figures are given in Table 2. Unfortunately, data was not available for several of these years.

The highest count was 97 in June 2005, and peaks in several other years were in late summer (July/August), all referring to low-water feeding. From 2016, there were regular high-water roosts in winter on the Lower Dark Water or adjacent field, with 36 in Nov 2016, the maximum.

## Bar-tailed Godwit

**Current Status:** An irregular spring passage migrant which may be seen flying east through the Solent in April and May (often with Whimbrel). Present in winter in small numbers at the mouth of the Beaulieu Estuary,

Bar-tailed Godwit – Road Bridge, April 2019

viewable from west of Inchmery House.

**Summary of Records:** Away from the mouth of the Beaulieu River, there were only a handful of winter records with 11 on 10th Jan 2010 being the highest single count. Autumn records were similarly infrequent, the last being a single individual in the fields behind the Coastguard Cottages on 9th Sept 2019. Most records over the twenty years were in spring and related to movement east through the Solent, the most significant being between 2nd and 11th May 2000, when 189 passed on five dates (98 on the 3rd); between 28th Apr and 3rd May 2004, when 84 passed on four dates; 67 on 23rd Apr 2005; and 67 on 3rd May 2007. Passage was lighter in the second decade with 20 on 15th Apr 2019, the most for that ten-year period.

## Black-tailed Godwit

**Current Status:** An irregular winter, spring, and autumn passage migrant seen in small numbers either on the Lower Dark Water (and visible from the road bridge) or on Stansore Pools. There is no low-water feeding east of the mouth of the Beaulieu River; beyond winter numbers can reach triple figures on both banks of the river.

**Summary of Records:** Recorded in every year apart from four (2009, 2011, 2016, and 2019). The months of the highest counts would suggest passage with 41 in Aug 2000 and 40 in Sept 2003.

A party of 32 in June 2002 were probably non-breeding. The only double-figure counts in the last decade were 18 in Feb 2013, ten in Feb 2012 and 2014, and 17 in Aug 2018.

## Turnstone

**Current Status:** A common winter visitor and passage migrant found almost exclusively feeding at low tide between the Coastguard Cottages and Stansore Point or at high-water roosts along the tide line to the east and west of the café, where they seem resilient to disturbance. The highest numbers likely are in autumn.

**Summary of Records:** Recorded in every year. Whilst winter populations seldom exceeded 50 in total (120 on 14th November being the exception), there were triple-figure counts for most autumns (August–October) with a day-maximum of 188 on 5th Oct 2013 – one more than on 19th Sept 2009.

See Table 2 for annual peak counts which mostly relate to high-water roosts.

## Knot

**Current Status:** A winter visitor and passage migrant, which may be seen in small numbers feeding along the foreshore between the café and the sluice gate, but where the winter population (November–February) is much higher at the mouth of the Beaulieu River.

**Summary of Records:** In the first decade the highest counts were in early spring and autumn with annual peaks of 60 on 10th Aug 2004; 84 on 21st Mar 2006; 130 on 13th Mar 2007; and 100 on 21st Mar 2009.

In the second ten-year period, apart from a party of 46 that flew across the Solent from the Isle of Wight and landed on shingle off Stansore Point before flying off west on 22nd Mar 2014, the annual maximum numbers given in Table 2 were of birds feeding and roosting on the mudflats to the west of Lepe House at the mouth of the Beaulieu River.

Numbers feeding there in 2020 increased from 91 in November, to 360 in January and to a day-maximum of 400 on 2nd March. Three on the foreshore at the road bridge on 6th May 2017 was the only summer record, whilst a solitary individual on the Dark Water and on Stansore Pools on four dates between 30th August and 7th December was unusual there.

## Ruff

**Current Status:** A rare spring and autumn passage migrant to Lepe.

**Pre-2000:** *One, 18th Sept 1997 (J Keddie).*

**All Records 2000–2020** (3): Three on 26th Mar 2002 (*JG Ross*), a male on the Dark Water on 21st Mar 2015 (*PF Fawkes*), and a juvenile on Stansore Pools on 5th Sept 2015 (*RA Chapman*) were all passage migrants.

## Curlew Sandpiper

**Current Status:** A scarce passage migrant.

**Pre-2000:** *One feeding on the foreshore on 11th May 1993 (RA Chapman).*

**All Records 2000–2020** (4): All were autumn passage migrants. One on 16th Sept 2012 (*PM Warne*); two feeding at low tide by the sluice gate on 28th Aug 2016 (*PF Fawkes*); one also by the sluice gate before flying east calling persistently on 15th Sept 2019 (*PF Fawkes*); and one at the mouth of the Beaulieu River, west of Inchmery House, between 1st and 4th Oct 2020 (*PF Fawkes*).

## Sanderling

**Current Status:** An irregular spring and autumn passage migrant most likely to be seen feeding along the tide line between the sluice gate and the café.

**Summary of Records:** Recorded in most years and whilst there were occasional winter sightings, the majority were in spring (May) and autumn (August–September). There were double-figure counts on 15th May 2005 (14), 25th May 2016 (19), and 7th Aug 2014 (24), whilst a party of 23 on 21st May 2018 fed along the tideline before departing east. There was similar evidence of spring passage that year when groups of six and nine flew east through the Solent on two dates in May. The only record away from the tideline was of two at Stansore Pools on 25th Aug 2016.

## Dunlin

**Current Status:** A winter visitor which now infrequently roosts at high tide along the beach, tending to fly to the Beaulieu River on the rising tide to avoid excessive disturbance. Feeds at low water between the sluice gates and the café, but rarely in numbers exceeding 50. Larger numbers feed on exposed mud to the west of Lepe House.

*Pre-2000: A low-tide count of 1,157 on 19th Jan 1998 was the highest on record and eclipsed all subsequent counts.*

**Summary of Records:** The last significant high-water roost in front of the café was in 2014 when there was a winter maximum of 520 on 25th January. Roosting numbers declined thereafter, even in the middle of winter. The peak feeding count in the decade 2010–2020 was 420 on 13th Mar 2016 with regular counts of 50 recorded in most winter months.

The highest count on the Dark Water was 13 on 30th Apr 2014 and on Stansore Pools, 17 on 7th Dec 2020. Feeding numbers at the mouth of the Beaulieu River (west of Lepe House) reached 450 in November 2020.

## Purple Sandpiper

**Current Status:** A winter visitor to Hampshire with a small but regular population at Southsea, and an occasional group at Barton-on-Sea. Always worth a close look through the Turnstones.

**All Records 2000–2020** (5): All were of single individuals in November and among roosting Turnstone on the foreshore: 3rd Nov 2003 (*JG Ross*), 22nd–27th Nov 2007 (*JG Ross & MC Adams*), 20th–22nd Nov 2008 (*MC Adams & S Sporne*), 16th–17th Nov 2015 (*K Coward & PF Fawkes*), and 2nd Nov 2020 (*R Chapman*).

## Little Stint

**All Records 2000–2020** (1): Two were feeding with Dunlin along the foreshore and seen from the road bridge on 19th Sept 2001 (*JG Ross*).

## Woodcock

*Pre-2000: One record, an adult with four chicks on the Dark Water Estuary on 8th May 1995 (D Unsworth).*

**All Records 2000–2020** (1): One at an unspecified location at Lepe on 18th Aug 2012 (*PD Jones*).

## Jack Snipe

**All Records 2000–2020** (2): Single individuals were flushed from the Dark Water on 11th Feb 2009 and 25th Oct 2014 (*JG Ross*).

## Common Snipe

**Current Status:** Winter visitor and passage migrant found mostly on the Dark Water and Stansore Pools, but accurate counts are difficult unless a warm sunny day entices them out into the open.

**Summary of Records:** The annual maximum count for most years between 2000 and 2020 is given in Table 2 and shows double-figure counts for the last nine years.

Numbers on the Dark Water reached 60 on 10th Mar 2001 and 50 on 27th Jan 2013, but these were eclipsed by a count of 92 on Stansore Pools on 25th Feb 2020, which probably included the Dark Water population as the water level there was extremely high.

Common Snipe
Dark Water Estuary, December 2020

The last spring departure date was 20th April (2013) and the first autumn return date was 15th July (2014).

## Grey Phalarope

**Current Status:** An annual late autumn migrant to the Hampshire coastline, usually following severe gales, but rarely more than ten individuals a year.

**All Records 2000–2020** (2): One on 15th Sept 2015 commuted twice between Stansore Pools, where

Grey Phalarope
Dark Water, September 2017

it was found (*K Coward*), and the Dark Water Estuary, before flying out into the Solent towards the Isle of Wight, and one was on the Dark Water in front of the hide from 9th to 12th Sept 2017 (*PF Fawkes*).

## Common Sandpiper

**Current Status:** A regular autumn passage migrant usually to be seen along the coastal wall east of Stone Point and the river that runs into the sluice by the road bridge.

**Summary of Records:** There were no winter records. The earliest spring date was 24th March (2014), the last autumn date, 27th September (2000). Whilst there were several records in April, the majority were in the early autumn with the highest counts being ten on 28th July 2000; 14 on 6th Aug 2003; eight on 19th July 2005; seven on 25th July 2006; and five on 30th July 2014.

## Green Sandpiper

**Current Status:** One or two are regular in winter in the Upper Dark Water, but otherwise only an occasional spring and autumn migrant.

**Summary of Records:** There were no records for any year between the dates of 3rd May and 7th July. The first winter record was not until 16th Dec 2012, but thereafter one or two were present on the Dark Water in most winters from mid-November to mid-March.

The highest counts were during the passage period, with six on 24th Aug 2015 and five on 12th Mar 2017 (four on passage and one regular winter bird). Autumn records from Stansore Pools included three on 23rd Aug 2016 and two on 20th Aug 2020.

## Lesser Yellowlegs

**All Records 2000–2020** (1): This rare American vagrant was present on Stansore Pools from 10th Nov 2013 to 13th Apr 2014 (*PF Fawkes*). It visited the Dark Water Estuary on 14th November and again on 22nd December (viewable from the road bridge) but otherwise it was loyal to the Stansore Pools.

It generated considerable interest from the twitching fraternity, being only the 14th record ever for Hampshire. Accepted by BBRC.

## Redshank

**Current Status:** An autumn passage migrant and winter visitor in small numbers to the Dark Water Estuary. It may also be seen feeding along the tide to the west of Lepe House and pairs are present on the Dark Water Estuary during the summer months.

**Summary of Records:** Table 2 gives double-figure annual maxima. Although present in winter on the lower reaches of the Dark Water Estuary, visible from the road bridge, the highest counts were in autumn, with 86 in Aug 2000, 73 in Aug 2005, and 49 in late July 2020. From 2015, low-water feeding counts at the mouth of the Beaulieu River included 36 in Dec 2016 and 43 in Oct 2020.

A pair was appearing to hold territory on 20th June 2011 and 10th Apr 2013 (Stansore Pools), but breeding was not proved. A pair did breed on the Dark Water in 2014, raising three young – the fourth in the clutch succumbing to a Sparrowhawk!

## Wood Sandpiper

**All Records 2000–2020** (2): Two on the Dark Water Estuary on 2nd July 2000 which were reported as being very vocal (*DJ Unsworth*) and one on 4th Aug 2002 (*PD Winter*).

## Spotted Redshank

**Current Status:** A winter visitor (one regularly on the Lower Dark Water Estuary) and occasional spring passage migrant.

**Summary of Records:** The first records were in 2000, with single individuals on 1st June 30th (the only June record in the twenty-year period) and 6th December, and then no more sightings reported until 11th Feb 2009. Thereafter, it was regularly recorded, with the highest numbers being four on 20th Apr 2013 and five on 16th Jan 2014, with three through until 6th April.

There was only one present during the winter months of 2017–2020. All records related to the Dark Water and there were no records for May or July, and only the one in June.

## Greenshank

**Current Status:** A regular autumn passage migrant in small numbers, with one or two wintering on the Dark Water Estuary and/or Stansore Pools.

**Summary of Records:** There were records for every year in the period 2000–2020. One or two wintered in most years, whilst spring and autumn passage was evident from records of four flying east on 3rd May 2000; four on 9th July 2003; six on 27th Aug 2004; five on 1st Sept 2009; and four on 21st Sept 2013. There were up to four between 20th Oct and 19th Nov 2020.

## Kittiwake

**Current Status:** Scarce on passage and in winter, and most likely seen in the Solent during and after strong winds.

**Summary of Records:** Thirteen years elapsed between the first record on 2nd Nov 2000 and the second on 12th Sept 2013. Thereafter, there were records in every year except 2016, including in spring, autumn, and winter, but probably only involving 25 individuals in total.

An adult lingered around the café and the Dark Water Estuary between 3rd and 25th Jan 2014 and seven flew west past Stansore Point on 5th Dec 2015, following a spell of particularly severe weather.

## Sabine's Gull

*Pre-2000 ONLY (1): Over the five days between 17th and 21st Oct 1987, following hurricane winds on the 15th–16th, Lepe/Needs Ore had its fair share of the 'wreck' with a highest day count on the 18th of 28+ in the Solent.*

## Black-headed Gull

**Current Status:** Seen all year round with the highest numbers likely in spring (February–March) and autumn. Breeds on Gull Island, but non-breeding individuals often present on the Dark Water Estuary.

**Summary of Records:** The three highest counts for the twenty-year period were 650 on Stansore Pools on 12th Mar 2016, 550 along the tide line on 1st Mar 2009, and 400 engaged in a feeding frenzy off the café on 24th Feb 2010.

**Lesser Yellowlegs**
*A long-staying visitor from America was present on
Stansore Pools over winter and early spring 2013/14*

## Little Gull

**Current Status:** A scarce spring and autumn passage migrant through the Solent, with occasional winter sightings.

**All Records 2000–2020** (13): Winter records included the exceptional sight of a party of 42 flying over Stansore Point and out into the mist on the Solent on 11th Nov 2013 (*W Borris*), whilst others included an adult flying west on 3rd Jan 2014 and another the same year that was on the water off the café from 13th to 16th February and which was joined by a first-winter individual on the 15th. In 2016, an adult was feeding on the Solent on 5th January and a first-winter flew west past Stone Point on 30th January, as did an adult on 19th November.

The only spring record was on 18th May 2017, whilst there were five autumn records which included single individuals from 17th to 22nd Oct 2006 and on 19th Sept 2011, two juveniles off the café from 12th to 15th Sept 2013, and a first-winter individual fishing off Coastguard Cottages on 22nd Sept 2017.

## Mediterranean Gull

**Current Status:** An increasingly numerous spring and autumn passage migrant, also occurring in smaller numbers in winter. Groups on passage can be found flying along the foreshore, resting on the tideline near the sluice gate, on the Dark Water Estuary or on Stansore Pools, and many adults will have their black hoods, especially in March and April.

**Summary of Records:** Recorded in all years 2000–2020 and whilst every month of the year was represented, rarely did day-maxima exceed ten during the winter months, whilst May and June numbers were fewer.

Adult Mediterranean Gull
in summer plumage – Lepe, May 2019

Annual maximum counts, given in Table 2 for years where numbers reached double figures, were during the spring (February–April, with an emphasis on March) and autumn (July–October).

These included counts of 100 on 2nd Mar 2013, 85 on Stansore Pools on 9th Feb 2015, and 145 on 4th Aug 2019, when there was a steady stream over the period of an hour leaving a night roost at the mouth of the Beaulieu River and flying east past Stone Point.

## Common Gull

**Current Status:** Whilst not as numerous as Black-headed Gull, there is usually a presence along the tideline at low water with the highest counts typically, but no longer exclusively, in the autumn (August–September).

**Summary of Records:** The annual maxima for those years where numbers reached double figures are given in Table 2. In the years 2000–2005, the highest annual count ranged from 94 (Aug 2000) to 160 (Aug 2005). Thereafter, peak numbers were lower and not confined to autumn, with 54 in Feb 2010 and 58 in Mar 2015.

## Great Black-backed Gull

**Current Status:** Regular on the Solent in winter and as a passage migrant, but rarely in numbers exceeding ten.

**Summary of Records:** Whilst there were double-figure counts for the first decade of the twenty-year period, with the day-maximum of 110 on 29th July 2004, they were thought to come from ploughed fields in the extreme north of the recording area.

Coastal records, whilst submitted in every year and for most months of each year, never involved more than ten on any one day.

## Herring Gull

**Current Status:** A common resident frequenting the tideline, but also seen in all months on the Dark Water Estuary and passing through the Solent in small numbers in spring and autumn.

**Summary of Records:** There was a paucity of records, with 20 on 6th Apr 2009 being the only significant record submitted. Two appeared to be 'pairing up' on the Dark Water Estuary in the spring of 2020, but there was no evidence of them breeding locally.

## Yellow-legged Gull

**Current Status:** Very scarce and likely only to be seen in autumn.

**All Records 2000–2020** (5): There were two between 12th and 17th Aug 2000, one on several dates from 16th July to 7th Sept 2001 (with two on 1st August), and an adult between 30th July and 7th Oct 2002. The last records were in 2003 and included the only one in spring (6th April – *PD Winter*) and what may have been the same individual adult on 3rd July, 7th August, and 3rd September.

All records were submitted by JG Ross, unless otherwise specified, and referred to the foreshore between the café and the road bridge.

## Lesser Black-backed Gull

**Current Status:** Whilst numerous in autumn and winter at certain inland localities in Hampshire, it is less numerous at coastal sites and may be described as a scarce passage migrant at Lepe, although probably under-recorded.

**All Records 2000–2020** (7): Three on 10th Aug 2000, two on 16th Apr 2001, one on 9th Nov 2002, and two on 19th Jan and 26th Feb 2003, which may have been the same individual, were the only records in the first decade. Thereafter, there was one on 25th Sept 2012, two from 22nd to 24th Apr 2013, and an adult, with a very dark mantle, present on and off by the road bridge between 28th Aug 2014 and 13th Jan 2015.

## Sandwich Tern

**Current Status:** An essentially summer visitor and passage migrant through the Solent, although increasingly present in ones and twos in winter. With an established breeding population at Lymington, individuals may be seen fishing off Lepe during May and June.

**Summary of Records:** Highest numbers related to movements east in April–May and west in September, the only double-figure counts being ten on 5th Sept 2011, 15 on 6th May 2017, 12 on 14th Sept 2018, and in 2019, 45 in an hour on 5th April, and 43 in an hour and a half on 15th April.

Four on 30th Dec 2020 was exceptional for the time of year, although there were singletons regularly recorded in winter from 2013.

## Little Tern

**Current Status:** Very scarce summer visitor and spring passage migrant, with a declining breeding population to the west at Lymington.

**Summary of Records:** Recorded in only nine of the twenty years and usually only in ones and twos, the exceptions being 18 passing east

through the Solent on 14th May 2005 and 17 in an hour and half, again east, on 30th Apr 2017.

The earliest arrival date was 7th April (2005) but there were no records for the autumn or winter, whilst the only record away from the open water was of an individual fishing on the Dark Water Estuary on 22nd May 2020.

## Roseate Tern

**Current Status:** Very scarce passage migrant at Lepe, with typically fewer than ten records a year in Hampshire.

***Pre-2000:*** *Two on 17th May 1993 (RA Chapman) and one on 20th May 1995 (JM Clark, GC Stephenson).*

**All Records 2000–2020** (3): There were two sitting on a buoy off the Coastguard Cottages for half an hour on 26th Apr 2015, one off Stansore Point on 10th September the same year, and one moving east through the Solent at a leisurely pace on 2nd May 2017 (*PF Fawkes*).

## Common Tern

**Current Status:** A common summer visitor and passage migrant through the Solent, with an established breeding population between Needs Ore and Lymington, from where individuals will fish off Lepe in the summer months.

**Summary of Records:** The earliest spring arrival date was 17th April (2003), and the latest departure date, 30th October (2004). The largest movements in spring and autumn through the Solent were 350 east on 21st May 2002 and 150 east on 9th Sept 2015. In 2017, 91 passed Stansore Point east in an hour on 30th April, 250 on 2nd May, and 44 on the 6th.

## Arctic Tern

**Current Status:** A scarce passage migrant, but not always easily distinguishable from Common Tern at a distance, so probably under-recorded.

**All Records 2000–2020** (5): On the Solent in autumn, with two east on 29th Aug 2001 (*ME Docherty*), three on 29th July 2004 (*JG Ross*), two on 19th Aug 2005 (*JG Ross*), one on 19th Sept (*P Matthews*), and one close to Stansore Point on 21st Sept 2013 (*JG Ross*).

## Black Tern

**Current Status:** There are surprisingly few sightings given the regular autumn passage down the Southampton Water and the numbers that pass Hill Head in July–September.

**All Records 2000–2020** (9): In the spring and early summer there were two on 27th Apr 2001 and singles on 17th June 2001 and 15th June 2010. The other six records were of birds on autumn passage through the Solent with three on 9th Aug 2004; one on 7th Aug 2010; two juveniles seen on several occasions between 9th and 15th Sept 2013; an adult on 31st Aug and 2nd Sept 2014; and the most recent, two on 21st Aug 2015.

## Great Skua

**All Records 2000–2020** (6): The first, and only spring record, was on 7th May 2012 (*PD Jones*), whilst the only autumn record was of an individual sitting on the water off the café for an hour on 18th Oct 2014 (*PM Warne*).

The other four records were in winter, with one flying west through the Solent on 20th Jan 2018 (*AD Ward*), one on the water off Coastguard Cottages (before chasing gulls towards the Beaulieu River) on 18th Dec 2019 (*PF Fawkes*), one flying from the Dark Water Estuary east over the café on 24th Feb 2019 (*PF Fawkes & P Jones*), and one passing east through the Solent on 21st Feb 2020 (*JK Andrews*).

## Pomarine Skua

**All Records 2000–2020** (4): All records referred to birds moving through the Solent. One pale-phase was recorded on 2nd Nov 2000 (*MA Litjens*), but fourteen years passed before the next two records, when one flew east on 6th May 2014 (*PM Warne*) and two passed west on 24th Oct 2014 (*PF Fawkes*). Five that flew east close to Stansore Point on 16th May 2019 (*PF Fawkes & A Woods*) were part of a movement of 17 seen passing along the east Solent coastline that day.

## Arctic Skua

**Current Status:** An irregular spring and autumn passage migrant flying east or west through the Solent, with May and September likely to be the peak times.

**Summary of Records:** With the exceptions of one on 27th Nov 2000, four chasing terns on 17th Aug 2004, two east through the Solent on 17th May 2013, and two passing Stone Point east on 18th May 2017, all records related to single individuals between the months of April and October. There were records for ten of the twenty years with May and September the peak months.

## Little Auk

*Pre-2000 ONLY (1): One flew east past the café on 6th Nov 1998, coinciding with an above average (13–14 individuals) influx of Little Auk along the Hampshire coast in November of that year.*

## Guillemot

**Current Status:** A scarce winter visitor (and occasionally on passage) that may be seen on, or flying through, the Solent. From a distance, not always distinguishable from Razorbill.

**Summary of Records:** In the first decade, several corpses were washed up including three on 6th Feb 2002. All sightings were on, or through, the Solent but numbering only ones and twos and almost exclusively in the winter months, the exceptions being

26th July 2004 and two September records (2009, 2017).

Two were close in shore on several dates between 2nd and 20th Jan 2014, as was an individual from 24th to 27th Nov 2015. There were only six records thereafter.

## Razorbill

**Current Status:** A scarce winter visitor (and occasionally on passage) through the Solent. From a distance, not always easy to identify from Guillemot.

**Summary of Records:** Most of the records, of which there were about twenty in total, were in winter, although there were several for September–October, and two for May (singles flying east in 2012 and 2014).

Although most often flybys, one was present close to shore off Stansore Point on several dates between 3rd and 24th Nov 2013, another was visible from the café from 7th to 10th Feb 2017, and a first-winter individual was close to the road bridge on 8th–9th Nov 2017.

## Black Guillemot

**Current Status:** A species more associated with north Scottish Islands than southern England where it is regarded as scarce.

**All Records 2000–2020** (1): A first-winter individual was at the mouth of the Beaulieu River, drifting east towards the Tower House, on 8th Jan 2018 (*PF Fawkes*). It was on

## Black Guillemot

*This 1st winter Black Guillemot is another
from Chris Button's sketch book*

view for little more than half an hour
and may well have been the same
individual seen off the Isle of Wight
in Nov 2017. There had been three
previous Hampshire records (1986,
1989, and 2010).

## Puffin

**All Records 2000–2020** (1): The
only record was of a heavily oiled
individual picked up off the beach
and taken into care at South Devon
Seabird Trust on 26th Nov 2000
(*K Talbot*). The corpse of a juvenile
was found on 15th Dec 2000.

## Red-throated Diver

**Current Status:** An uncommon winter
and passage migrant, and only likely
to be seen on, or flying through, the
Solent.

**All Records 2000–2020** (7): All records
were between November and January.
The first was on 23rd Dec 2001
(*JG Ross*) and it may have been the
same individual found oiled and
washed up dead a month later.

The second, also seen by Jeff Ross
flying through the Solent, was on
22nd Jan 2003, which was followed
by two fishing offshore on a falling

tide on 25th Nov 2007 (*R Souter*). Thereafter, there were singles on 20th Nov 2011 (*P Jones*), 2nd Jan 2014 (*W Borras*), 8th Nov 2014 (*PF Fawkes*), and 26th–27th Nov 2015 (*PF Fawkes*), which was close off Stansore Point affording long and excellent views.

## Black-throated Diver

**Current Status:** An uncommon winter visitor and passage migrant on, or through, the Solent.

**All Records 2000–2020** (6): The first record was on 9th Nov 2000. It was over a decade before the second, this off Stansore Point on 26th Dec 2013.

There were three records in 2018: singletons off Gull Island (mouth of the Beaulieu River) on 9th January, flying west through the Solent on 17th April, and on the water off the café on 23rd November.

The last sighting for the twenty-year period was off Stansore Point on 30th Oct 2019.

## Great Northern Diver

**Current Status:** Whilst still not a common winter visitor off Lepe, there are more records than for the other two divers combined and it has become more regular and longer staying over the past two or three

Great Northern Diver – Solent off Coastguard Cottages, December 2020

years, most often frequenting the stretch of water between Stone Point and the entrance to the Beaulieu River.

**Summary of Records:** Before 2014, there were records of single individuals on one or two dates in 2001, 2002, 2003, 2006, 2011, and 2013. In 2014, two were regularly present between 5th January and 20th March, which set the trend for long-staying individuals over the winter months.

Whilst 2nd June 2015 was an unseasonal date, records thereafter were more typical, with at least one present for parts of each winter between 2015 and 2020: 26th Nov–13th Dec 2015; 24th Nov–9th Dec 2017; 24th–28th Feb and 6th–24th Dec 2018; 8th–30th Nov 2019; 1st Jan–15th Mar 2020; and in 2020, two from 7th to 31st December.

## European Storm Petrel

**Current Status:** Rare off Lepe, but occasional storm-driven individuals seen in autumn and winter to the west (Milford-on-Sea) and the east (Hayling Island).

*Pre-2000 (1): One on 1st May 1988 was the only spring record in Hampshire that year.*

**All Records 2000–2020** (2): The first was a storm-driven individual on 2nd Nov 2000 (*MA Litjens*), whilst the second, on 27th May 2006, was Lepe's contribution to an unprecedented spring influx (c.130, mostly moving west) along the Hampshire coast from mid-to-late May.

## Fulmar

**Current Status:** No longer a common spring and autumn passage migrant to the west Solent, and nor, therefore, to Lepe, and mostly associated with stormy weather.

*Pre-2000: A storm-blown bird in Jan 1998, which had been ringed in Orkney, was rehabilitated at Devon Seabird Trust and released in August of that year.*

**All Records 2000–2020** (3): One flew east close to the shoreline on 6th Sept 2014 (*AR Collins*), one flew east past the café on 3rd May 2015 (*PF Fawkes*), and an individual was seen to circle the Dark Water Estuary and fly west towards the Beaulieu River on 3rd May 2019 (*PF Fawkes*).

## Manx Shearwater

*Pre-2000 ONLY (1): (2): Singles on 19th Sept 1987 and 3rd Nov 1996, both west through the Solent.*

## White Stork

**All Records 2000–2020** (1): An individual was on the Dark Water Estuary for the morning of 8th Sept 2002 (*JG Ross*).

## Gannet

**Current Status:** The odd individuals may 'loaf about' the Solent between Stansore Point and the Beaulieu River in early and late winter, but the most likely time to witness movement is between May and August.

Gannet
Over the Solent off the café

Sightings off Lepe tend be weather dependent (the stormier the better) and passage is rarely heavy, unlike to the east off Hill Head and to the west off Milford-on-Sea.

**Summary of Records:** There were records in every year except 2009, with December being the only month over the twenty-year period that was not represented.

Day counts rarely reached double figures, the exceptions being 37 passing east in two hours on 7th July 2012 and 19 moving west in half an hour on 5th May 2015.

A party of 45 sitting on the Solent off the café on 11th Aug 2015 was an unusual sight.

## Cormorant

**Current Status:** Present in small numbers, typically one to four, throughout most of the year on the Solent and occasionally on the Dark Water Estuary.

**Summary of Records:** Highest numbers were recorded in late autumn, when 31 on 28th Oct 2001, 20 on 19th Oct 2013, and 26 on 17th Oct 2014. A party of 67 that flew up from a small reservoir behind Stansore Pools (private site) on 1st Jan 2012, was an exceptional number and date (*JG Ross*).

## Shag

**Current Status:** Uncommon at Lepe, as it is generally on this stretch of the Solent.

**All Records 2000–2020** (6):
All sightings were off Stansore Point and presumably involved the same individual(s) on each occasion: 3rd–13th Jan 2014 (with two there on the 3rd); 3rd–13th Dec 2015; 5th Jan and 9th Feb 2016; 19th Nov 2018; and 15th Jan 2020.

## Spoonbill

**Current Status:** Once rare, but now more common along the Solent coastline. There has been a regular presence in winter of a dozen or so on mudflats off Needs Ore, and these

## Spoonbills

*Doing what they do best, standing around - this time just down the road at Keyhaven.*

Spoonbill

Hampshire
10ᵗ January 20

preening
yellow edged
Spatulate bill

yellowish
breast band

Sturdy thick
black legs

can be seen from as far east as the café – albeit through a scope! Better views may be obtained from west of Lepe House.

**Summary of Records:** Between 2000 and 2016, there were only six records. All were of single individuals, the first on 2nd July 2000 (*JG Ross*), and except for one on the Dark Water from 13th to 16th Sept 2001, all were flyovers.

From 2016, records from the epicentre of Lepe increased and included two flying past the café on 6th Aug 2017; one on Stansore Pools on 25th Feb 2018 and again from 2nd to 5th March; five on the Dark Water on 11th Dec 2018; and three there from 4th to 18th Aug 2020.

## Bittern

**Current Status:** A rare winter visitor, but there is suitable habitat in the upper reaches of the Dark Water Estuary, so patience could be rewarded.

Bittern
Dark Water Estuary, March 2017

*Pre-2000: One on the Dark Water Estuary 1st Jan–7th Feb 1994 (M Cannings & IJ Wilton).*

**All Records 2000–2020** (2): Both records were from the north end of the Dark Water Estuary. These were on 10th Jan 2010 (*JG Ross*) and

12th Mar 2017 (*PF Fawkes*), the latter hunting and preening out in the open in the mid-afternoon sun.

## Grey Heron

**Current Status:** Typically, one to four around during the winter months, usually present on the Dark Water Estuary and/or Stansore Pools, but also along the coastline at low tide.

**Summary of Records:** The highest count was 12 on 11th Aug 2000 and on 6th June 2015, when on the latter occasion eight flew over Stansore Point from the Cadland Estate and crossed the Solent early morning, leaving three on Dark Water and one on Stansore Pools.

In addition to a seemingly unattached individual roaming between the Dark Water and Stansore Pools, a pair was present on the upper reaches of the Estuary in early spring of 2020, with a juvenile there on 4th August.

## Great White Egret

**Current Status:** In extending its range north from the Mediterranean, it is no longer a rarity in Hampshire and so there is the increasing likelihood of seeing the occasional bird at Lepe, probably on the Dark Water in late summer/early autumn.

**All Records 2000–2020** (6):  The first record was as early as 2005 (when regarded a British Rarity) seen flying from Stone Point to Cowes on 23rd July (BirdGuides).

It was almost a decade before the second record, a single individual

Great White Egret
Dark Water Estuary, September 2016

on the Dark Water for several hours and visible from the road bridge on 7th Oct 2014 (*PF Fawkes & PD Winter*).

There were singletons, thereafter, on 17th Sept 2016 (Dark Water), 30th Oct 2017 (Stansore Pools), 23rd June 2019 (Dark Water, viewable from the road bridge), and on several dates between 30th Aug and 11th Sept 2020.

## Little Egret

**Current Status:** The frequency of records has been steadily increasing over the twenty-year period in line with county and national trends and it is now a common resident found anywhere along the tideline at low water, on the Dark Water Estuary, or on Stansore Pools.

Its numbers are higher in autumn and winter, typically ten to fifteen on any one day.

**Pre-2000:** *The first ever record for Lepe was on 15th Nov 1993.*

**Summary of Records:** Recorded in a variety of habitats and in every month of every year over the two decades. The annual maxima are given in Table 2 and show that the highest counts were in autumn, with 29 on 23rd Aug 2005, 25 on 30th Sept 2009, and 20 on Oct 2020. Typically, numbers declined in May/July to fewer than five on any one day, although there were ten on 26th June 2020.

## Osprey

**Current Status:** A regular autumn passage migrant to the Solent that may occasionally be seen fishing on the Dark Water and commuting between Lepe and the Beaulieu River.

**Summary of Records:** There were only a handful of records during the period 2000 to 2010 with one on 8th Oct 2000; two from 29th Aug to 1st Sept 2002; and in 2004, one on 10th April and one on 27th August. There were regular sightings on the Dark Water in every year from 2010, predominantly from mid-August to mid-October, mostly of single individuals and invariably visible from the road bridge. The exceptions to this were two spring/summer records on 24th May 2019 and 1st June 2020, and two together on 20th Sept 2011 and 22nd Oct 2016.

## Honey Buzzard

**Current Status:** A rare breeding species in Britain, with the New Forest remaining one of its strongholds.

**All Records 2000–2020** (2): One flew south west on 19th Sept 2011 (*AJB Lester*) and one flew south east from the Dark Water Estuary, over the café and out into the Solent on 7th Sept 2016 (*PF Fawkes*). Both were adults and both were on passage.

## Sparrowhawk

**Current Status:** An uncommon resident that may occasionally be seen circling over the Cadland Estate, or around East Hill Farm, both being potential breeding sites.

**Summary of Records:** Inexplicably, the only record before 2014 was on 27th Feb 2011. The handful of records each year post-2014 were mostly in the autumn (August to October). Exceptions were a male taking a Redshank chick off Stansore Pool on 9th June 2014; a female over Stansore Pools on 21st Apr 2016; a male crossing to the Solent on 31st Jan 2018; and one at Lepe Farm on 4th Dec 2018. One over the Dark Water on 8th October was the only record in 2019, but there were three in 2020, with a pair being very vocal on 31st August, and a female over the Dark Water Estuary on 5th September and Stansore Pools on the 13th.

## Goshawk

**Current Status:** The recent increase in records no doubt relates to birds wandering from territories on the Cadland and Exbury Estates. Its success this century as a breeding species in the New Forest has been meteoric.

**Summary of Records:** Prior to 2016, records were exclusively from the north end of the Dark Water Estuary at East Hill, where single individuals were seen on 16th Aug 2005, 10th Aug 2013 (with two present on 7th September), and 24th Aug 2015.

Records were more numerous post-2016, a trend repeated throughout the New Forest and wider afield, with several sightings from the road bridge and from behind the Coastguard Cottages. 50% of the records were between August and September and included the occasional juvenile.

## Marsh Harrier

**Current Status:** One or two may be seen regularly between October and March quartering the reed beds on the Dark Water. The best vantage points are from the road bridge, from the field adjacent to the Coastguard Cottages or from the hide. There appears to be daily movement between Lepe and Calshot/Fawley in one direction, and Lepe and Needs Ore, in the other.

**Summary of Records:** There were single records in several years between 2000 and 2013, mostly between October and March, and of single birds over the Dark Water.

There were two records in 2014, one of which was at Stansore Pools at the time of the Lesser Yellowlegs. From 2015, there were multiple sightings in every year, mostly from the road bridge looking north.

In 2018 a pair was present from 12th March, hatching two young in June. One juvenile was seen regularly with the female up until 12th December. There was no suggestion of breeding in 2019 and 2020, despite regular sightings during the winter months and early spring.

Noteworthy at the time was an individual flying east through the Solent on 18th Apr 2015 and two males (with possibly a third) and a female together over the Dark Water on 11th Oct 2019.

## Hen Harrier

**Current Status:** An increasingly scarce winter visitor to Hampshire and to the New Forest, and rare at Lepe.

**All Records 2000–2020** (3): In 2010, a male was seen over snow-covered fields to the west of Gardeners Cottage on 10th January (*JG Ross*) and a ringtail was present on the Dark Water Estuary for several hours on 8th March (*S Clemons et al.*). The third record was in 2011, a ringtail on 24th December near East Hill Farm above the Dark Water Estuary (*R Whitehead*).

## Red Kite

**Current Status:** With the recent expansion south and into Hampshire

from its stronghold in the Chilterns, future sightings of this species may be anticipated.

**All Records 2000–2020** (9): There were four in the spring/early summer and five in the autumn/early winter. In the first decade, there were

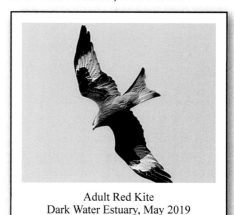

Adult Red Kite
Dark Water Estuary, May 2019

three sightings of single individuals on 7th Oct 2000 (*DJ Unsworth*), 17th Aug 2005 (*R Severs*), and 14th Oct 2010 (*AC Johnson*).

There were two records for 2013, one at East Hill Farm on 22nd May 2013 (*JG Ross*), the other over the Dark Water Estuary on 22nd November (*PF Fawkes*).

Thereafter, one was seen by the coast road on 18th Mar 2015 (*AR Collins*), one lingered over Stansore Pools and the Cadland Estate for an hour on 14th Sept 2018, and in 2019, two drifted over the Dark Water on 1st April and one flew up the Dark Water Estuary on 3rd May (*PF Fawkes*).

## Buzzard

**Current Status:** A regular, almost daily, sight of up to six soaring over Cadland Estate and/or the Dark Water Estuary, where breeding is suspected.

**Summary of Records:** There were regular sightings of up to four in all years, mostly from the Dark Water Estuary and surrounding fields and viewable from behind the Coastguard Cottages, but also over the Cadland Estate and seen from Stansore Point.

Breeding was suspected in the grounds of the two principal estates, but not proved. All double-figure counts, taken when walking the Lepe Loop and therefore prone to possible duplication, were in the spring with 15 on 6th Apr 2012, the day-maximum.

## Barn Owl

**Current Status:** It appears that it is no longer resident at either of the two farms (Lepe and East Hill) and is now extremely scarce at Lepe.

**Summary of Records:** There are several records of single individuals for the winter months (late October–early April) in 2001, 2003, and 2004, and for July and August in 2003. There was a sighting at dusk near Lepe Farm on 6th Nov 2014 and over the Dark Water, clearly visible from the road bridge, on 2nd Oct 2020, which constitute the only records in the nine years between 2011 and 2020.

## Little Owl

**All Records 2000–2020** (2): There was one in a tree to the east of Stone Point on 7th June 2000 that was being mobbed by Chaffinches (*JG Ross*) and one at an undisclosed site on 5th Mar 2006 (*AL Lewis*).

## Short-eared Owl

**All Records 2000–2020** (1): One was seen quartering the reeds and grassland at Stansore Pools on 30th Oct 2011 (*MJ Smith*).

## Tawny Owl

**Current Status:** Likely to be resident and breeding in woods around East Hill Farm and Lepe Farm.

**All Records 2000–2020** (7): Heard calling during daylight hours at East Hill Farm on 19th Jan 2011 (*AS Rhodes*); along the boardwalk on the Reserve on 5th Oct and 20th Nov 2014 (*PF Fawkes & JG Ross*); in the grounds of Inchmery House on 28th Dec 2014 (*PF Fawkes*); and from different parts of the Dark Water Estuary on 16th Sept 2015, 11th Mar 2016, and 30th Sept 2019.

## Hoopoe

***Pre-2000 ONLY*** *(2): Singles on 25th Apr 1994 (I Lawrence) and 24th Apr 1997 (JM Keddie).*

## Kingfisher

**Current Status:** Resident during the winter months on the Dark Water Estuary, where often visible from the road bridge and/or on Stansore Pools. Breeds along riverbanks in the New Forest, so unlikely to be seen at Lepe from April to August.

**Summary of Records:** Recorded regularly in every year, with most sightings between mid-August and early-March, but with several 'one-off' records for May, June, and July, although no suggestion of breeding within the recording area.

Mostly one or two, but there were four on 17th Aug 2002 and three on 21st Sept 2013, 8th Sept 2015, and 11th Sept 2019, all probably relating to post-breeding dispersals.

## Wryneck

**All Records 2000–2020** (2): One disappeared into shrubbery behind the top car park at the café on 14th Sept 2013 (*AR Collins*) and one was seen for a couple of hours in scrub at Stansore Point on 17th Sept 2016 (*PF Fawkes*).

## Lesser Spotted Woodpecker

**All Records 2000–2020** (3): Singles on 30th June and 3rd July 2000, 15th June 2001, and 16th Jan 2015 – all between the horse field above the Lower Dark Water and East Hill Farm (*JG Ross*).

## Great Spotted Woodpecker

**Current Status:** Resident, but not numerous. Individuals or pairs may be seen or heard throughout the year on the Lepe Loop (Lepe and East Hill Farms), on the Reserve and at Stansore Pools.

Great Spotted Woodpecker
Lepe Farm Cottages, May 2020

Breeding population Is estimated to be in the range of three–six pairs.

**Summary of Records:** Six on 20th June 2011 was the highest count on any one day. There was little information on numbers in May/June.

## Green Woodpecker

**Current Status:** Resident but not as frequently recorded as Great Spotted Woodpecker. May be encountered inland along the Lepe Loop (East Hill Farm), but more often heard in the woods than seen.

## Summary of Records:

Ten on 4th Aug 2004 was an exceptional number, whilst the only breeding record was in 2011.

## Kestrel

**Current Status:** Occasionally encountered at Stansore and on the Dark Water, but more frequently over the fields near East Hill and Lepe Farm. It is unlikely that there are more than two pairs within the recording area.

**Summary of Records:** There were regular winter records of both sexes from the Dark Water Estuary and Stansore Point.

A male Kestrel with prey
Stansore Point, September 2019

During the breeding season, a pair was present in June 2013 and a pair was seen in courtship display in March 2020 over the fields at the junction of Exbury and Inchmery Road. Breeding was not proved in either case.

## Merlin

**Current Status:** A scarce winter visitor to Hampshire, but it may be encountered along the coastline at Lepe particularly when there is an abundance of small waders.

**Summary of Records:** There were records for twelve of the twenty years, involving a total of 15 individuals, with most between late October and mid-March.

Although there was a relatively long-staying individual on the Dark Water Estuary between 21st and 28th Oct 2010, most sightings were of birds passing through the recording area, often at speed.

## Hobby

**Current Status:** A summer migrant that breeds in small numbers in the New Forest, so the occasional late summer/autumn sighting at Lepe would not be unusual.

**Summary of Records:** Singles were seen at Lepe in eleven of the twenty years possibly involving as many as 17 individuals.

Nine records were from August/ September, but there were spring and summer records, mostly from the Dark Water Estuary, in 2003 (15th May), 2004 (21st June), 2005 (17th May), 2015 (30th May), and 2018 (24th April).

## Peregrine Falcon

**Current Status:** One or two pairs breed locally and so individuals may occasionally enter the recording area, particularly at the mouth of the Beaulieu River.

**Summary of Records:** There were records for every year except 2009, with every month represented except June. Most were singles, although there were occasions when two were seen, and on 17th Jan 2017 three were involved in aerial combat over the mouth of the Beaulieu River.

Most sightings were along the shore between Inchmery and Stansore Point, with greater frequency to the west of Coastguard Cottages.

## Jay

**Current Status:** Resident, and whilst rarely seen along the foreshore, individuals are likely to be encountered on the Lepe Loop. There is no documentation on the breeding population, but it is unlikely that there are more than three pairs within the recording area.

**Summary of Records:** Seven were counted within the recording area on 10th May 2013, the highest number for any one day. Otherwise, records of one or two in woodland at East Hill, around Lepe Farm and on the southern fringes of the Cadland Estate to the east of Stansore Point.

Jay – East Hill, October 2018

## Magpie

**Current Status:** A resident, occasionally seen on the Dark Water Estuary or the Stansore Pools but more often on farmland along Exbury Road and at East Hill.

**Summary of Records:** No records were submitted for the period 2000–2020.

## Jackdaw

**Current Status:** A resident found in a variety of habitat but mostly in the fields on the Lepe Loop.

**Summary of Records:** No meaningful records were submitted over the twenty years.

## Rook

**Current Status:** Not common near the shoreline and there are no known rookeries away from the two Estates.

**Summary of Records:** There was a record of 100 on 25th Aug 2013, but where precisely was not documented.

## Carrion Crow

**Current Status:** A common resident most frequently seen on and around the fields on the Lepe Loop and in numbers often exceeding 50 on Stansore Pools in early spring.

**Summary of Records:** The highest count was 300 on 25th Feb 2013, but there were very few other records submitted for the twenty-year period.

## Raven

**Current Status:** Once rare in the County, pairs now breed locally to Lepe, so there is an increasing frequency of individuals seen, or heard calling, as they fly over any part of the recording area.

**Summary of Records:** Although one or two were seen in most years in the first decade, with four on 4th Oct 2008, there were only a handful of records for each of those years. From 2014, the numbers of records per year were well into double figures. Whilst most were in winter there were two May records, one as late as 31st (2008). There were no sightings in June or July. Nine flying west along the tideline on 28th Jan 2019 reflected the dramatic change in its status both in Hampshire and at Lepe over the twenty-year period.

## Coal Tit

**Current Status:** Resident, with a breeding population estimated at between five and ten pairs. A frequent winter visitor to the feeders by the hide, it may also be seen in the conifer trees in the top car park, behind Coastguard Cottages, and along the coastal path and road to Inchmery.

## Marsh Tit

**Current Status:** The least common of the Tits resident at Lepe (Bearded Tit is not of the same family) and whilst breeding is suspected, it has not yet been proved. A regular visitor in winter to the hide feeders.

## Blue Tit

**Current Status:** The breeding population within the recording area is probably in the range of 25–35 pairs. Numbers are augmented in spring and autumn whilst winter parties in double figures are likely to be encountered in suitable habitat.

## Great Tit

**Current Status:** The breeding population is likely to be between 15 and 25 pairs. It is not as common on passage, or in winter, as Blue Tit and Long-tailed Tit but is a regular visitor to the hide feeders.

## Bearded Tit (Reedling)

**Current Status:** Whilst regarded as a 'scarce passage migrant and winter visitor' to Hampshire, the developing reed beds on the Upper Dark Water might prove increasingly attractive over time.

**All Records 2000–2020** (1): One was calling from the reed beds on the Dark Water Estuary on 22nd Oct 2010 (*MA Litjens*).

## Woodlark

**Current Status:** Whilst breeding in suitable habitat in the New Forest and as close as Badminston Common, it remains a rarity at Lepe.

**All Records 2000–2020** (1): One in the camping field behind the café on 28th Dec 2020 (*JG Ross*).

## Skylark

**Current Status:** The likely breeding population is estimated at between three and five pairs in crop fields around Lepe Farm and East Hill Farm. Numbers may be augmented in winter after a spell of very cold weather or in autumn by passage migrants.

**Summary of Records:** A flock of 25 on 10th Jan 2010 was associated with a cold-weather movement, whilst 30 passing east off Stone Point in one hour on 20th Oct 2015 were on passage.

## Sand Martin

**Current Status:** An early summer visitor (mid-March), but passage in spring is minimal. There is no breeding locally, so often absent in May/July, but frequently seen in numbers over the Solent during autumn passage.

**Summary of Records:** The earliest arrival date was 16th March (2020). The highest autumn counts were 200 on 24th Aug 2000 and, as part of a massive hirundine movement ahead of a weather front (cf. Swallow), a minimum of 200 passed Stone Point flying east on 22nd Sept 2016. There was only one October record, that of a single individual on the 1st in 2000.

## Swallow

**Current Status:** A spring and autumn passage migrant. Typically, fewer than five pairs breed and only around the farmsteads at Lepe and East Hill.

**Summary of Records:** The earliest date was 31st March (2002).

Otherwise, most records were from the second week in April. Typically, spring passage was small with 75 on 2nd May 2014 and 40 on 24th Apr 2005 being the highest day counts.

Autumn movements east were much more impressive with a count, ahead of a weather front, from Stone Point of 3000 in 45 minutes on 22nd Sept 2016 (cf. Sand Martin and House Martin).

Other triple-figure counts were mostly in September and lasting no longer than an hour and half. These included 900 on 13th Sept 2015, 1000 on 29th Sept 2015, 600 on 17th Sept 2016, and 700 on 14th Sept 2018.

The largest October movement involved 250 on the 17th in 2015, and there were two November sightings, the last on 19th (2013).

## House Martin

**Current Status:** A spring and autumn passage migrant often seen on the Dark Water or on the Solent but not known to breed at Lepe.

**Summary of Records:** The earliest arrival date was 4th April (2007) and the latest departure date was 18th October (2020).

Spring passage over the twenty-year period was minimal.

However, autumn passage, starting in most years in late August and peaking in September, was epitomised by several triple-figure counts, which included 500 over the Solent on 6th Sept 2014, with 200 on wires behind Coastguard Cottages on the 14th; a build-up of 300 in reed beds on the Dark Water on 3rd Sept 2017; and a movement north across the Solent from the IOW of 1500 in one hour on 14th Sept 2018.

## Cetti's Warbler

**Current Status:** A resident in small numbers and frequently heard all year from scrub on the Dark Water and along the coastal path from Stansore to the Cadland Estate.

The estimated breeding population is in the range of 8–12 pairs and is anticipated to increase.

**Summary of Records:** The first record was on 29th June 2001. Thereafter, there were numerous records for every year and in all months of each year, with typically one–two singing males in May/June, but four pairs holding territory in 2005 and 2015.

## Long-tailed Tit

**Current Status:** Parties (often mixed with other members of the Tit family and with Goldcrest) may exceed 20 during autumn passage and in the winter months.

Whilst there is no documentation on the breeding population, it is scarce during the summer and confined to the wooded areas of the Lepe Loop.

Yellow-browed Warbler
Stansore Point, October 2015

Juvenile Long-tailed Tit, one of thirteen
Top Fields, May 2019

## Wood Warbler

**All Records 2000–2020** (1): One (in the company of Aquatic Warbler) in scrub along the foreshore between the DD Monument and the Cadland Estate on 21st Aug 2018 (*PF Fawkes*).

## Yellow-browed Warbler

**All Records 2000–2020** (2): One calling at the edge of the pony field in the Reserve on 9th Nov 2014 (*PF Fawkes*) and one by the path at Stansore on 15th Oct 2015 (*PF Fawkes*).

## Willow Warbler

**Current Status:** A regular autumn migrant, but scarce in the spring and usually absent in the breeding season.

**Summary of Records:** The earliest spring record was 19th April (2014). A migrant in full song along the coastal path on 2nd Sept 2020 was most unseasonal. The highest autumn day counts were in 2020, when there were 20 at Stansore on 5th September and ten there on the 13th.

## Chiffchaff

**Current Status:** A common summer resident and autumn migrant which may also be present during the winter months in suitable habitat along the coastal path or the boardwalk on the Reserve.

The breeding population within the recording area is estimated to be in the range of 25–35 pairs.

**Summary of Records:** There were records for all months, with four on 26th Nov 2016 the highest single count in winter. Triple-figure day counts in autumn included 40 between the café and Cadland Estate on 6th Oct 2017, 35 on 30th Sept 2019 (when there was 65% coverage of the recording area), and 30 on 20th Aug 2020.

## Aquatic Warbler

**All Records 2000–2020** (1): One in scrub along the foreshore between the D-Day Monument and the Cadland Estate on 21st Aug 2018 was visible, on and off, for twenty minutes (*PF Fawkes*). Accepted by BBRC.

## Sedge Warbler

**Current Status:** A summer migrant breeding in small numbers, typically two–five pairs, in reed beds on the Dark Water Estuary.

**Summary of Records:** The earliest arrival date was 16th April (2004), the latest departure date was 7th October (2014). There were autumn records of one to four from Stansore Pools, but very little significant data was available from the records submitted.

## Reed Warbler

**Current Status:** A summer migrant breeding in small numbers, now typically in the range of two–five pairs in reed beds on the Dark Water Estuary and at Stansore Pools.

**Summary of Records:** The earliest arrival date was 13th April (2005). The number of breeding territories declined over the twenty-year period from 15 singing males in 2005, to eight in 2011, and to six in 2015. There was evidence of small autumn passage with the latest recorded date being 8th September (2015).

## Grasshopper Warbler

**All Records 2000–2020** (1): One at Stansore Pools on 28th Aug 2017 (*PF Fawkes et al.*).

## Blackcap

**Current Status:** A common summer visitor breeding across the recording area in numbers estimated to be between 25 and 35 pairs. Autumn passage increases the population in August/September.

**Summary of Records:**
The only overwintering record was 11th Dec 2005. Otherwise, the earliest arrival date was 21st March (2014). There were 18 singing males across the whole area in 2011, ten in 2015 over 75% of the recording area, and ten along the Dark Water Estuary alone in 2018.

The highest migrant count at one locality only (Reserve) was 18 on 28th Aug 2017. There were several late October records and two in November, with singles on the 3rd (2016) and the 7th (2004).

## Garden Warbler

**Current Status:** A scarce summer visitor with breeding generally confined to one or two pairs on the Reserve and/or Dark Water Estuary.

**Summary of Records:** There were records of one or two singing males in May/June in thirteen of the twenty years from 2000 to 2020, with three holding territory in June 2000, but the only confirmed breeding was of a pair on the Reserve in 2014. The earliest arrival date was 24th April (2010) and the latest departure date was 28th August (2017).

## Lesser Whitethroat

**Current Status:** A summer visitor, typically arriving mid-April and with one–three territories most often held between the café and the Cadland Estate, but also on the Reserve and opposite Lepe Farm Cottages.

**Summary of Records:** The earliest spring record was 17th Apr (2015). There was recorded singing in eight of the summers between 2000 and 2014 and in all summers thereafter, with four territories in 2016 between the café and the Cadland Estate and three in 2020 over the whole recording area. The latest departure date was 4th October (2019).

## Common Whitethroat

**Current Status:** A common summer resident, arriving from mid-April onwards, with likely small autumn passage in September. Breeding territories may be found in suitable habitat over the whole study area, with a population estimated to be in the range of 15–30 pairs.

**Summary of Records:** The earliest arrival date was 17th April (2004) and there were records for every year with 14 territories held in 2011 and 15 singing males recorded on the 8th May 2020. The highest autumn passage count was 17 on 5th Sept 2020 at Stansore Point. The latest recorded date before winter departure was 3rd October (2015).

## Dartford Warbler

**Current Status:** With breeding pairs as close to Lepe as Badminston Common, winter dispersal to coastal sites is not unexpected, although there is little suitable habitat, even in winter, away from Stansore Pools.

***Pre-2000:*** *Breeding was confirmed in 1999 when a pair with three young were seen on 1st June.*

**Summary of Records:** Although there were June records in 2000 (3, 25th) and 2001 (4, 20th), breeding was not confirmed.

Dartford Warbler
Stansore Pools, August 2017

There were no records at Lepe between 11th Dec 2005 and 21st Feb 2014, but there were in the subsequent three years.

In 2015, there was one at Stansore on 15th Aug and 23rd Oct 2015, and probably a different individual in gardens at Coastguard Cottages on 20th October. There were just two records in 2016, both at Stansore, and one on the early date of 28th July, whilst there was one present at Stansore Pools between 26th Aug and 9th Nov 2017.

There were no records for 2018/19, but in 2020 there were singles at Stansore on 16th October, at the road bridge on 19th November, and possibly the same individual in the top fields on the 27th.

## Firecrest

**Current Status:** Increasingly common resident in small numbers (1–3) in autumn and winter. The most suitable habitat is found along the boardwalk, around the café and in the wood at East Hill Farm. Breeding within the recording area is anticipated.

**Summary of Records:** There were no records in the first decade, the first being on 25th Nov 2010.

From 2013, there were records for every year, mostly of one–three between October and February, although there were sightings in March, August, and September.

Indeed, a singing male in the wood at East Hill Farm on 28th May 2019, followed by a family party of five along the boardwalk on 1st Sept 2020, raised the possibility of breeding within the recording area. The highest number of adults on any day was five on 1st Nov 2015.

## Goldcrest

**Current Status:** A resident, with an estimated breeding population in the range of 15–25 pairs, and a passage migrant in small numbers.

**Summary of Records:** The highest daily count was 20 on 9th Nov 2014 along the coastal path between the café and Stansore Pools. There was little information available on the breeding population over the twenty-year period.

Firecrest
Reserve Boardwalk, October 2020

## Wren

**Current Status:** A common resident found in suitable habitat across the study area but with little data available. The likely breeding population, given the extent of suitable habitat, is estimated to be in the range of 60–80 pairs.

Nuthatch at East Hill Farm – February 2019

## Nuthatch

**Current Status:** A dearth of records would suggest that this species is not common at Lepe. This may be the case along the coastal stretch, but it may be heard calling from the southern edge of the Cadland Estate, at the back of Lepe House and at East Hill Farm.

## Treecreeper

**Current Status:** Regular along the boardwalk and in woods between Lepe House and Inchmery House, but little historical data was available, with no reference made to the breeding population.

## Rose-coloured Starling

**All Records 2000–2020** (1): A juvenile was present between the Coastguard Cottages and the Dark Water Estuary from 20th to 26th Oct 2010 (*L Gwynn et al.*) spending much of its time sitting on overhead wires with the local Starling population.

## Starling

**Current Status:** Common resident with the highest concentration in the late summer following post-breeding dispersal. There are no local roosts (so no murmuration at dusk) nor large-scale wintering numbers. The breeding population is not high and is estimated to be in the range of 10–15 pairs, mostly at sites away from the coastal path.

## Blackbird

**Current Status:** A resident with an estimated breeding population in the range of 30–40 pairs.

**Summary of Records:** There was little data available other than a record from 2011 of 16 adults observed in suitable breeding habitat in June.

## Fieldfare

**Current Status:** A winter visitor (November–March) which may appear in large feeding flocks anywhere which is suitable within the recording area but most likely on the Lepe Loop.

**Summary of Records:** Whilst recorded in fourteen of the twenty years, the number of day records for each year was remarkably few.

The earliest winter arrival date was of one along the meadows near Stansore on 16th Oct 2015, whilst the latest departure date was 7th April (2013). Most records involved large flocks in the fields around East Hill Farm and during the months of November to March. These included 100 on 12th Dec 2004, 150 on 23rd Dec 2006, and 50 on 8th Feb 2009.

Closer to the coast, there was a flock of 55 on the lower reaches of the Dark Water Estuary on 10th Mar 2015, 150 in bushes at the edge of the camping field on 20th Nov 2017, and 50 on the Reserve on 23rd Nov 2019.

## Redwing

**Current Status:** A winter visitor (October–March) which is unlikely to be encountered along the coastal stretch but may be present in the surrounding fields in small numbers.

**Summary of Records:** The only double figure counts were in 2013, when there were flocks of 25 on the Dark Water Estuary on 25th February and ten in fields north of Lepe House on 7th April, and in 2016 when there was a group of ten along Stanswood Road on 9th February.

## Song Thrush

**Current Status:** A common resident, but little historical data available.

The estimated breeding population in the recorded area is in the range of 20–30 pairs.

## Mistle Thrush

**Current Status:** A resident and most likely observed in fields behind the Coastguard Cottages and on the 'Loop' walk, particularly around East Hill Farm and Lepe Farm.

The estimated breeding population is in the range of two–five pairs.

**Summary of Records:** There were very few records submitted besides family groups of 16 on 3rd Aug 2004, 14 on 1st July 2009 and 26 on 18th July 2010.

## Spotted Flycatcher

**Current Status:** An autumn passage migrant in small numbers that may be seen anywhere over the recording area but traditionally behind the Coastguard Cottages or at Stansore.

**Summary of Records:** There were no spring records, but one in the wood below East Hill Farm on 28th May 2019 was the only sighting outside of August/September.

Spotted Flycatcher
Boardwalk, September 2019

There were records of one–four for all years between 2010 and 2020, the earliest autumn date for a passage migrant being 24th August (2015) and the latest departure date, 25th September (2004).

## Robin

**Current Status:** The breeding population, now estimated at between 30 and 40 pairs, is likely to be augmented during autumn passage and in winter.

**Summary of Records:** In 2011, 20 adults were recorded in suitable habitat in April, of which 14 were thought to be holding territory in June, but there was a lack of historical data.

## Nightingale

**Current Status:** Now a scarce spring passage migrant having once bred at Stansore and on the Reserve.

**Summary of Records:** One singing on 14th Apr 2000 was not heard again and was presumably a migrant. Breeding was likely in 2001, when a male was holding territory in Allwoods Copse (Cadland Estate) between 8th April and 20th June. In 2005, there was a singing male heard on 23rd April and two on 6th May, but breeding was not proved, as was the case in 2012 when one was singing on the 7th and 27th May. There were only two records thereafter, singles in song east of Stone Point on 20th May 2013 and 20th Apr 2014.

## Pied Flycatcher

**All Records 2000–2020** (1): A female outside the hide on 4th Aug 2018 (*PF Fawkes*).

## Black Redstart

**Pre-2000:** *A female was around Stone Farm on 19th Oct 1995 (BJ Pinchen).*

**All Records 2000–2020** (1): One on 16th Nov 2002 (*R Ship*), but the locality within the recording area was not reported.

## Redstart

**Current Status:** There is a healthy breeding population in the New Forest, but its status at Lepe is best described as 'a scarce autumn migrant'.

**Summary of Records:** Records numbered fewer than 30, with none between 2000 and 2010. The majority were from late August into September and mostly of single individuals, although there were three at Stansore Point on 1st Sept 2015.

There was one spring record, a male on 27th Apr 2015, whilst the latest departure date was 28th September (2020). A juvenile on 6th July 2014 would lend support to suspicions that pair(s) bred close to the recorded area.

## Whinchat

**Current Status:** An occasional spring migrant, but more likely to be seen sitting on fence posts on the Dark Water Estuary or at Stansore in August and September.

**Summary of Records:** There were records in fifteen of the twenty years, 75% of which were in September, mostly of single individuals, and rarely involving more than three or four individuals a year.

During spring passage, there were three on 25th Apr 2005 and single individuals in May in 2004 (13th), 2016 (3rd), and 2019 (2nd). The earliest autumn return date was July 27th (2015), whilst in the same year, three were present at Stansore between 31st August and 3rd September. The latest departure date was 3rd October (2017).

## Stonechat

**Current Status:** Typically, one–four present on the Dark Water Estuary and/or Stansore Pools between October and February, with higher numbers present in the late autumn when on passage.

**Summary of Records:** Two pairs bred in 2000 (five young, 5th May and two young, 30th June). This was the last year that breeding was proved, although there were two pairs seen in May/July in 2001, three in 2002, two in 2003, and one in 2004.

The only May/July record thereafter was a male on the Dark Water Estuary in 2020.

Although there were four at Stansore on 7th Aug 2020, most sightings were from late September until February, with 20th April (2008) the last spring date outside of those years when present through the summer. Double-figure day counts of ten on 2nd Oct 2014 and 12 on 4th Oct 2019 were of passage migrants.

Female Stonechat on Stansore Pools 2018

There were records daily through the winter in all years, mostly at Stansore Point and on the Dark Water.

## Wheatear

**Current Status:** A spring and autumn passage migrant that may be seen in ones or twos between late March to mid-May and again from mid-August to early October, most commonly flitting along the coastal path or in the fields above the Dark Water Estuary.

**Summary of Records:** The earliest arrival date was 16th March (2013). Other years when there was a March record were 2004 (28th), 2014 (19th), and 2016 (28th).

Although records in spring were far fewer than in autumn there was a day-maximum of six on 1st May 2000, 12 on 22nd Apr 2014, and seven on 3rd Apr 2015. There were several mid-May records, but none for June.

The earliest date for return passage was 12th July (2004) the latest date for departure was

30th October (2004). The bulk of the autumn records were from mid-August to early October, the highest count being nine on the Dark Water on 24th Sept 2009.

## House Sparrow

**Current Status:** Once scarce, small flocks (10–15) are now regular in winter at four sites where there is bramble and scrub. They are along the coastal path in front of Inchmery House, in the car park at Coastguard Cottages, at Lepe Farm Cottages, and less frequently, on Stansore Pools. More information is required on its breeding status at Lepe which is currently estimated at between three and eight pairs.

**Summary of Records:** Five on 1st July 2009, one on 4th Mar 2010, four on 28th Aug 2010, and one on 20th Apr 2013 were all considered worthy of placing on record, such was its scarcity within the recording area in the first decade. Thereafter, records became more numerous with winter flocks at four favoured localities often exceeding ten.

## Dunnock

**Current Status:** A common resident found across the recording area where there is bramble and scrub, with an estimated breeding population in the range of 20–30 pairs.

**Summary of Records:** There was little data available, but 16 territories were documented in 2011, whilst a day-maximum of 25 on 2nd Sept 2014, all at Stansore, was indicative of autumn passage.

## Yellow Wagtail

**Current Status:** A scarce spring passage migrant, but not uncommon in small numbers in the autumn between mid-August and late September.

**Summary of Records:** The only two spring records were four on 25th Apr 2001 and one on 24th Apr 2014. The first autumn passage return was 19th August (3, 2002), whilst the latest date for departure was 26th September (2015). Recorded most years and predominantly in September with double-figure day counts of 20 on 1st Sept 2007, 13 on 4th Sept 2003, and a group of 37 flying west over the Dark Water Estuary on 14th Sept 2016.

## Grey Wagtail

**Current Status:** An irregular winter visitor in ones and twos, most often seen at Stansore or on the Dark

Grey Wagtail
Stansore Pools, September 2018

Water Estuary. In autumn, passage migrants may be seen or heard flying east over Stone Point.

**Summary of Records:** There were records for most years in the twenty-year period, predominantly between October and March. There were single records for May (1, 2020), June (1, 2000), July (1, 2002), and August (1, 2010). All September sightings were of passage migrants off Stone Point, with a day-maximum of 18 on 13th Sept 2015.

## Pied Wagtail

**Current Status:** A resident, inhabiting the coastline and farmlands. The breeding population is estimated at between five and ten pairs. Numbers at Lepe are augmented in the autumn by passage migrants.

**Summary of Records:** There was little data for the twenty-year period outside of counts of birds on passage during September and October. Double-figure counts of migrants passing Stone Point early morning included 35 on 4th Oct 2008, 31 on 13 Sept 2015, 30 on 11th Oct 2015, and 30 on 19th Oct 2018.

## White Wagtail

**Current Status:** A sub-species of Pied Wagtail often referred to us an 'alba' wagtail. An uncommon spring migrant, but probably overlooked in autumn when it becomes more difficult to distinguish from Pied Wagtail.

**All Records 2000–2020** (7): Five of the six records were in spring with single individuals on 16th Apr 2004 (*JG Ross*), 10th May 2013 (*PM Warne*), and 31st Mar 2019 (*PF Fawkes*); and two on 14th Mar 2015 (*AR Collins,*) and 17th Mar 2020 (*PF Fawkes*).

The only autumn records were of two on 25th Sept 2000 (*JG Ross*) and 23rd Aug 2014 (*PF Fawkes*).

## Meadow Pipit

**Current Status:** The small resident population is augmented during autumn migration, with late-September–October being the peak period of passage.

**Summary of Records:** Double-figure day counts included 80 on 29th Sept 2014 (50 in fields behind Coastguard Cottages and 30 distributed along the Dark Water Estuary), 30 on 14th Oct 2015, and 60 at Stansore Pools on 16th Oct 2020.

## Tree Pipit

**Current Status:** An uncommon spring and autumn passage migrant, but often reliant on call to distinguish from Meadow Pipit.

**All Records 2000–2020** (6): Unquestionably under-recorded. There were two spring records, with singles on 16th Apr 2006 (*JG Ross*) and 18th Apr 2015 (*PF Fawkes*).

The four autumn records were of birds flying east over Stone Point calling and included three on 13th Sept 2015, three on 17th Sept 2016, and single individuals on 28th Aug 2017 and 2nd Sept 2020.

## Water Pipit

**Current Status:** An occasional winter visitor and spring passage migrant which may be seen on the Dark Water Estuary or at Stansore Pools.

**Summary of Records:** In 2005, a long-staying individual was on the Dark Water from 28th February to 17th April. Other winter records, again of single individuals, included 6th Jan and 23rd Nov 2013, 4th Dec 2017, 9th Feb 2016, 4th Dec 2017, and 14th Nov 2018. Most records referred to spring passage migrants (March/April), with five in summer plumage on the Dark Water on 18th Apr 2019. The one autumn record was on 23rd Oct 2005.

## Rock Pipit

**Current Status:** One or two may be seen between October and March anywhere along the coastline, but most likely from Stone Point east.

**Summary of Records:** There were records for every year and with breeding pairs holding territories in 2002 and 2003, every month was represented up until 2010. Thereafter, except for seven at Stansore on 13th Sept 2012, records were exclusively between October and March and rarely more than three on any one day. The last spring date was 17th March (2019), the first winter return was 4th October (2015).

## Chaffinch

**Current Status:** A common resident found across the recording area, with a breeding population estimated in the range of 50–60 pairs.

**Summary of Records:** There was little data for the period, other than a count in April 2011 of 31 territories in tetrad SZ49P for the Hampshire Bird Atlas.

## Brambling

**Current Status:** Although winter flocks in double-figure numbers are to be found in the south-west corner of the New Forest, it is a scarce autumn migrant to Lepe but may easily be overlooked on passage.

**All Records 2000–2020** (5): There was an exceptional record of 30 in fields to the west of Gardeners Cottage on 30th Nov 2005, with 12 still present on 19th December (*JG Ross*), but thereafter records involved birds moving through the recording area. There were two on 17th Jan 2006 (*JG Ross*); single individuals at Coastguard Cottages on 22nd Oct 2010 (*MA Litjens*) and the Meadows on 17th Nov 2015 (*PF Fawkes*); and two flying east past Stansore Point on 30th Oct 2019 (*PF Fawkes*).

## Hawfinch

**Current Status:** Whilst likely to be present on the Exbury and Cadland Estates, and probably around East Hill Farm, it is scarce along the Lepe coastline and over the recording area generally.

**All Records 2000–2020** (4): Eleven years elapsed between the first record of a single individual on 5th Mar 2006 in East Hill Copse (*JG Ross*) and the next of two along the sea wall east of Stone Point on 1st Dec 2017 (*PF Fawkes*). Thereafter, four were seen to come in off the Solent at Stansore Point on 6th Jan 2018 (*PF Fawkes*), with what was presumably one of those present in the vicinity of the upper car park on 31st January and 6th February (*S Clemons*), whilst two flew west along the coastal path on 19th Oct 2019 (*R Chapman*).

## Bullfinch

**Current Status:** Seen all year in pairs or small family parties, most frequently on or around the Reserve, but in other suitable habitats on the Lepe Loop. The estimated breeding population across the recording area is between five and ten pairs.

A male Bullfinch – Reserve Boardwalk, February 2020

**Summary of Records:** There were records for all years, most months of each year and across the recording area, but most from the Reserve and behind the upper car park at the café. The highest day counts were ten on 1st Nov 2005 and 5th Jan 2020, but there were numerous groups of six to eight in winter, whilst May/ June records in four successive years (2011–2015) suggested breeding.

## Greenfinch

**Current Status:** A resident whose numbers are likely to be augmented in autumn by grounded passage migrants. It is showing signs of recovery as a breeding species at Lepe with a current estimated population of 10–15 pairs.

**Summary of Records:** There was little data available other than nine breeding territories plotted in 2011 in TTV SZ49P, and four territories within a three-hundred-yard radius of the café in 2019.

## Linnet

**Current Status:** A resident with a breeding population of between seven and ten pairs, mostly confined to Stansore and scrub between Coastguard Cottages and East Hill copse. Numbers increase at Lepe during autumn when there may be passage east past Stone Point and flocks grounded.

Linnet – Stansore Pools, May 2019

**Summary of Records:** A flock of 225 on 3rd Feb 2015 was an exceptional winter count. Most double-figure counts relate to grounded autumn passage migrants at Stansore, with 50–70 on 16th–28th Aug 2014, 100 on 1st Aug 2015, 40 on 18th Sept 2016, and 50–60 on 11th–18th Sept 2020. There were five breeding territories recorded in June 2011 (SZ49P).

## Lesser Redpoll

**Current Status:** Irregular winter visitor to the Reserve and Dark Water Estuary.

**Summary of Records:** Except for 25 coming in off the Solent and viewed from Stone Point on 6th Jan 2018, most records were in October/ November and related to small parties on or over the Reserve. Double-figure counts included 12 on 13th Nov 2013, ten on 20th Oct 2015, and 12 on 17th Oct 2017.

## Goldfinch

**Current Status:** A common resident and autumn passage migrant, with early-morning easterly movement off Stone Point likely in late-September– October when conditions are favourable. Winter numbers tend to be low, but the estimated breeding population within the recording area is in the range of 20–30 pairs.

**Summary of Records:** There were few records before 2014, after which there were regular counts at Stone Point in the first two hours of light.

In 2015, a minimum of 870 flew past the Point over four days between 30th September and 20th October, with a day-maximum of 420 on the 11th October, whilst in 2017, 120 were grounded in fields behind Coastguard Cottages. 80 passed east over Stansore on 19th Oct 2018 and 120 on 16th Oct 2020.

## Siskin

**Current Status:** An irregular winter visitor but early-morning watches from Stone Point in the autumn would likely reveal passage east when the conditions are favourable.

**Summary of Records:** There was a group of 20 on 19th Oct 2003, and 15 on 18th Oct 2006 along the

Siskin.– Hide Feeders, September 2019

upper reaches of the Dark Water Estuary, and May/June records from habitat towards East Hill Farm in 2012, 2013, and 2015, but most data referred to autumn migration with passage east past Stone Point. In 2015, on ten early mornings between 8th September and 11th October, a total of 683 flew over, with a maximum day count of 220 during the first hour of light on 30th September.

## Snow Bunting

***Pre-2000:*** *A female was photographed on 19th Nov 1995 (JK Andrews & PE Hutchins).*

**All Records 2000–2020** (1): A male flew over the Coastguard Cottages calling on 3rd Jan 2014 (*PF Fawkes*).

## Yellowhammer

**Current Status:** Although still breeding locally (one–two pairs on Badminston Common), it is now a rare sighting at Lepe.

**Summary of Records:** Singing males were recorded in 2000 (5, 29th May–30th June); 2002 (2, 23rd June); 2003 (5, 15th May); 2004 (2, 25th March); and 2005 (3, 10th May–23rd June). Fourteen years elapsed before the next record, one above the cliff between the café and Stansore Point on 16th Oct 2019.

## Reed Bunting

**Current Status:** Resident in small numbers and mostly seen on the Dark Water Estuary and at Stansore Pools where the combined breeding population is thought to be between five and eight pairs.

**Summary of Records:** There were winter records of one or two in most years, with a maximum in one group of ten on 10th Jan 2010. The breeding population on the Dark Water Estuary steadily declined from ten males holding territory in 2007 to three in 2020.

# Table 1

## Annual Winter (Oct-April) Maxima for Selected Wildfowl and Great Crested Grebe

| | early 2000 | 2000-01 | 2001-02 | 2002-03 | 2003-04 | 2004-05 | 2005-06 | 2006-07 | 2007-08 |
|---|---|---|---|---|---|---|---|---|---|
| **Brent Goose** | **560** | **670** | **550** | **407** | **328** | **337** | **300** | **166** | **15** |
| Maxima seen on | May-08 | Apr-01 | Mar-07 | Apr-18 | Mar-27 | Oct-16 | Apr-14 | Oct-18 | May-05 |
| **Teal** | | **70** | **415** | **60** | **120** | **80** | **120** | **50** | **108** |
| Maxima seen on | | Oct-31 | Jan-14 | Feb-01 | Nov-02 | Dec-05 | Nov-13 | Oct-08 | Nov-03 |
| **Eider** | | **6** | **14** | **45** | **25** | **9** | **150** | **80** | **36** |
| Maxima seen on | | Apr-30 | Mar-23 | Mar-19 | Mar-04 | Apr-03 | Apr-14 | Dec-23 | Nov-24 |
| **Red-breasted Merganser** | **12** | | **10** | **10** | **12** | **15** | **4** | **6** | **6** |
| Maxima seen on | Mar-31 | | Dec-23 | Mar-28 | Mar-03 | Nov-07 | Mar-05 | Apr-07 | Jan-05 |
| **Great Crested Grebe** | | **10** | **20** | **17** | **25** | **14** | **10** | **6** | **9** |
| Maxima seen on | | Nov-18 | Dec-Jan | Apr-04 | Nov-24 | Nov-07 | Dec-21 | Dec-23 | Jan-05 |

Data was not readily available for those months where figures are not given.

| 2008-09 | 2009-10 | 2010-11 | 2011-12 | 2012-13 | 2013-14 | 2014-15 | 2015-16 | 2016-17 | 2017-18 | 2018-19 | 2019-20 | late 2020 |
|---|---|---|---|---|---|---|---|---|---|---|---|---|
| **310** | | **200** | **300** | **450** | **500** | **620** | **544** | **286** | **105** | **150** | **270** | **254** |
| Nov-20 | | Oct-20 | Oct-30 | Feb-25 | Oct-16 | Mar-06 | Feb-25 | Mar-11 | Apr-08 | Mar-19 | Oct-30 | Oct-18 |
| **120** | **90** | **5** | **30** | **103** | **420** | **42** | **45** | | **32** | | | **70** |
| Dec-06 | Mar-04 | Feb-27 | Mar-24 | Dec-01 | Nov-24 | Oct-14 | Dec-19 | | Oct-01 | | | Nov-17 |
| **1** | | **40** | **3** | | **5** | **5** | **5** | **14** | **12** | **5** | **9** | **1** |
| Jan-Apr | | Nov-21 | Jan-20 | | Dec-07 | Apr-08 | Nov-28 | Mar-23 | Jan-06 | Nov-28 | Feb-05 | Novc 19 |
| **2** | **2** | **3** | **4** | **7** | **4** | **8** | **5** | **2** | **4** | **2** | | **1** |
| Apr-04 | Mar-04 | Feb-27 | Feb-11 | Feb-25 | Mar-12 | Dec-28 | Jan-25 | Feb-07 | Dec-11 | Feb-24 | | Nov-27 |
| **57** | **10** | **8** | | | **18** | **9** | **23** | **9** | | **9** | **6** | **8** |
| Jan-10 | Jan-10 | Nov-21 | | | Dec-26 | Nov-10 | Nov-26 | Dec-11 | | Mar-19 | Jan-05 | Dec-06 |

# Table 2

## Annual Maxima for Selected Waders, Gulls and Egrets

| | 2000 | 2001 | 2002 | 2003 | 2004 | 2005 | 2006 | 2007 |
|---|---|---|---|---|---|---|---|---|
| **Oystercatcher** | 64 | 135 | 175 | 121 | 174 | 170 | 102 | |
| Maxima seen in | June | Mar. | Sept | Feb. | Mar. | Mar. | July | |
| **Lapwing** | 80 | 50 | 37 | 67 | 200 | 100 | 50 | 65 |
| Maxima seen in | Dec | Aug | June | Dec | Dec | Nov | Dec | Feb |
| **Grey Plover** | 93 | 57 | 101 | 130 | 78 | 181 | 63 | 56 |
| Maxima seen in | Aug | Jan | Sept | Dec | Sept | Jan | Sept | Jan/Sept |
| **Ringed Plover** | 67 | 53 | 80 | 100 | 70 | 35 | 49 | |
| Maxima seen in | Oct | Sept. | Dec. | Sept | Oct. | Aug. | Oct. | |
| **Curlew** | 55 | 36 | 41 | 32 | 84 | 97 | | |
| Maxima seen in | Oct | Aug | Aug | July | July | June | | |
| **Turnstone** | 100 | 78 | 82 | 107 | 115 | 140 | 103 | 87 |
| Maxima seen in | Sept | Sept | Sept | Oct | Sept | Oct | Oct | Nov |
| **Knot** | | 29 | 16 | | 60 | | 84 | 130 |
| Maxima seen in | | Feb | Aug | | Aug | | Mar | Mar |
| **Common Snipe** | 17 | 60 | 10 | 30 | 12 | 8 | | |
| Maxima seen in | Dec | Mar | Jan | Jan | Ferb | Mar | | |
| **Redshank** | 86 | | 23 | 40 | 45 | 73 | 47 | |
| Maxima seen in | Aug | | Aug | Nov | Sept | Aug | Sept | |
| **Mediteranean Gull** | | | 10 | | 25 | | 34 | |
| Maxima seen in | | | Mar | | Apr | | Mar | |
| **Common Gull** | 94 | 125 | 125 | 119 | 115 | 160 | | |
| Maxima seen in | Aug | Sept | Sept | Sept | Aug-Sept | Aug | | |
| **Little Egret** | 20 | 7 | 24 | 11 | 20 | 29 | 16 | 18 |
| Maxima seen in | Aug | May | Sept | Aug | Aug | Aug | Oct | Sept |

Data was not readily available for those months where figures are not given.

| 2008 | 2009 | 2010 | 2011 | 2012 | 2013 | 2014 | 2015 | 2016 | 2017 | 2018 | 2019 | 2020 |
|---|---|---|---|---|---|---|---|---|---|---|---|---|
|  | 64 | 100 |  |  |  | 100 | 102 |  |  | 105 |  | 95 |
|  | Nov. | Feb. |  |  |  | Aug. | Aug. |  |  | Sept. |  | Oct. |
|  |  | 80 |  | 25 | 250 |  | 60 | 214 |  |  | 151 |  | 95 |
|  |  | Nov |  | July | Dec |  | Dec | Nov |  |  | Dec |  | Nov |
|  |  |  |  |  |  | 35 | 32 |  | 124 | 95 | 140 | 60 |
|  |  |  |  |  |  | Mar | Nov |  | Feb | Oct | Jan | Jan |
|  | 105 |  |  |  | 40 | 65 | 180 | 120 |  | 96 |  |  |
|  | Sept. |  |  |  | Dec. | Oct. | Oct. | Aug. |  | Oct. |  |  |
|  |  |  |  |  |  | 38 |  | 36 |  |  | 14 |  |
|  |  |  |  |  |  | Jan |  | Nov |  |  | July |  |
| 138 | 187 | 104 | 165 | 135 | 188 | 145 | 127 | 140 | 155 | 119 | 79 | 142 |
| Sept | Sept | Aug | Oct | Sept | Oct | Aug | Sept | Aug | Aug | Aug | Aug | Oct |
|  | 100 | 20 | 40 |  |  |  |  |  |  | 145 | 38 | 400 |
|  | Mar | Jan | Dec |  |  |  |  |  |  | Feb | Jan | Mar |
| 7 | 11 | 8 |  | 42 | 50 | 26 | 21 | 11 | 25 | 49 | 45 | 92 |
| Nov | Feb | Mar |  | Dec | Jan | Mar | Feb | Oct | Oct | Dec | Dec | Feb |
|  | 28 |  |  |  |  | 10 |  | 36 |  | 45 |  | 49 |
|  | Oct |  |  |  |  | Mar |  | Dec |  | Aug |  | July |
| 81 | 84 | 42 | 20 | 40 | 100 | 54 | 85 | 45 | 30 | 55 | 145 | 95 |
| Mar | Feb | Feb | July | Mar | Mar | Sept | Feb | Mar | Sept | Aug | Aug | Oct |
|  | 10 | 54 |  |  |  | 47 | 58 | 18 |  |  | 12 | 26 |
|  | Mar | Feb |  |  |  | Dec | Mar | Aug |  |  | Aug | Feb |
| 6 | 25 | 13 | 4 | 10 | 14 | 16 | 13 |  |  | 13 | 4 | 20 |
| Oct | Sept | Aug | Oct | July | Sept | Jan | Sept |  |  | Aug | Mar | Oct |

**Brent Goose, Brant Goose**
*Branta bernicla*

**Dark-bellied Brent Goose**
*Branta bernicla bernicla*

**Pale-bellied Brent Goose**
*Branta bernicla hrota*

**Black Brant**
*Branta bernicla nigricans*

**Red-breasted Goose**
*Branta ruficollis*

**Canada Goose**
*Branta canadensis*

**Barnacle Goose**
*Branta leucopsis*

**Greylag Goose**
*Anser anser*

**European White-fronted Goose, Greater White-fronted Goose**
*Anser albifrons*

**Greenland White-fronted Goose**
*Anser albifrons flavirostris*

**Mute Swan**
*Cygnus olor*

**Egyptian Goose**
*Alopochen aegyptiaca*

**Shelduck, Common Shelduck**
*Tadorna tadorna*

**Mandarin Duck**
*Aix galericulata*

**Garganey**
*Spatula querquedula*

**Shoveler, Northern Shoveler**
*Spatula clypeata*

**Gadwall**
*Mareca strepera*

**Wigeon, Eurasian Wigeon**
*Mareca penelope*

**Mallard**
*Anas platyrhynchos*

**Pintail, Northern Pintail**
*Anas acuta*

**Teal, Eurasian Teal**
*Anas crecca*

**Tufted Duck**
*Aythya fuligula*

**Scaup, Greater Scaup**
*Aythya marila*

**Eider, Common Eider**
*Somateria mollissima*

**Velvet Scoter**
*Melanitta fusca*

**Common Scoter**
*Melanitta nigra*

**Long-tailed Duck**
*Clangula hyemalis*

**Goldeneye, Common Goldeneye**
*Bucephala clangula*

**Goosander, Common Merganser**
*Mergus merganser*

**Red-breasted Merganser**
*Mergus serrator*

**Red-legged Partridge**
*Alectoris rufa*

**Grey Partridge**
*Perdix perdix*

**Pheasant, Common Pheasant**
*Phasianus colchicus*

**Nightjar, European Nightjar**
*Caprimulgus europaeus*

**Swift, Common Swift**
*Apus apus*

**Cuckoo, Common Cuckoo**
*Cuculus canorus*

**Stock Dove**
*Columba oenas*

**Woodpigeon, Common Wood Pigeon**
*Columba palumbus*

**Turtle Dove, European Turtle Dove**
*Streptopelia turtur*

**Collared Dove, Eurasian Collared Dove**
*Streptopelia decaocto*

**Water Rail**
*Rallus aquaticus*

**Moorhen, Common Moorhen**
*Gallinula chloropus*

**Coot, Eurasian Coot**
*Fulica atra*

**Little Grebe**
*Tachybaptus ruficollis*

**Red-necked Grebe**
*Podiceps grisegena*

**Great Crested Grebe**
*Podiceps cristatus*

**Slavonian Grebe, Horned Grebe**
*Podiceps auritus*

**Black-necked Grebe**
*Podiceps nigricollis*

**Oystercatcher, Eurasian Oystercatcher**
*Haematopus ostralegus*

**Avocet, Pied Avocet**
*Recurvirostra avosetta*

**Lapwing, Northern Lapwing**
*Vanellus vanellus*

**Golden Plover, European Golden Plover**
*Pluvialis apricaria*

**Grey Plover**
*Pluvialis squatarola*

**Ringed Plover, Common Ringed Plover**
*Charadrius hiaticula*

**Little Ringed Plover**
*Charadrius dubius*

**Whimbrel, Eurasian Whimbrel**
*Numenius phaeopus*

**Curlew, Eurasian Curlew**
*Numenius arquata*

**Bar-tailed Godwit**
*Limosa lapponica*

**Black-tailed Godwit**
*Limosa limosa*

**Turnstone, Ruddy Turnstone**
*Arenaria interpres*

**Knot, Red Knot**
*Calidris canutus*

**Ruff**
*Calidris pugnax*

**Curlew Sandpiper**
*Calidris ferruginea*

**Sanderling**
*Calidris alba*

**Dunlin**
*Calidris alpina*

**Purple Sandpiper**
*Calidris maritima*

**Little Stint**
*Calidris minuta*

**Woodcock, Eurasian Woodcock**
*Scolopax rusticola*

**Jack Snipe**
*Lymnocryptes minimus*

**Snipe, Common Snipe**
*Gallinago gallinago*

**Grey Phalarope, Red Phalarope**
*Phalaropus fulicarius*

**Common Sandpiper**
*Actitis hypoleucos*

**Green Sandpiper**
*Tringa ochropus*

**Lesser Yellowlegs**
*Tringa flavipes*

**Redshank, Common Redshank**
*Tringa totanus*

**Wood Sandpiper**
*Tringa glareola*

Spotted Redshank
*Tringa erythropus*

Greenshank, Common Greenshank
*Tringa nebularia*

Kittiwake, Black-legged Kittiwake
*Rissa tridactyla*

Sabine's Gull
*Xema sabini*

Black-headed Gull
*Chroicocephalus ridibundus*

Little Gull
*Hydrocoloeus minutus*

Mediterranean Gull
*Ichthyaetus melanocephalus*

Common Gull, Mew Gull
*Larus canus*

Great Black-backed Gull
*Larus marinus*

Herring Gull, European Herring Gull
*Larus argentatus*

Yellow-legged Gull
*Larus michahellis*

Lesser Black-backed Gull
*Larus fuscus*

Sandwich Tern
*Thalasseus sandvicensis*

Little Tern
*Sternula albifrons*

Roseate Tern
*Sterna dougallii*

Common Tern
*Sterna hirundo*

Arctic Tern
*Sterna paradisaea*

Black Tern
*Chlidonias niger*

Great Skua
*Stercorarius skua*

Pomarine Skua, Pomarine Jaeger
*Stercorarius pomarinus*

Arctic Skua, Parasitic Jaeger
*Stercorarius parasiticus*

Little Auk
*Alle alle*

Common Guillemot, Common Murre
*Uria aalge*

Razorbill
*Alca torda*

Black Guillemot
*Cepphus grylle*

Puffin, Atlantic Puffin
*Fratercula arctica*

Red-throated Diver, Red-throated Loon
*Gavia stellata*

Black-throated Diver, Black-throated Loon
*Gavia arctica*

Great Northern Diver, Common Loon
*Gavia immer*

Storm Petrel, European Storm Petrel
*Hydrobates pelagicus*

Fulmar, Northern Fulmar
*Fulmarus glacialis*

Manx Shearwater
*Puffinus puffinus*

White Stork
*Ciconia ciconia*

Gannet, Northern Gannet
*Morus bassanus*

Cormorant, Great Cormorant
*Phalacrocorax carbo*

Shag, European Shag
*Phalacrocorax aristotelis*

Spoonbill, Eurasian Spoonbill
*Platalea leucorodia*

Bittern, Eurasian Bittern
*Botaurus stellaris*

Grey Heron
*Ardea cinerea*

Great White Egret, Great Egret
*Ardea alba*

Little Egret
*Egretta garzetta*

Osprey, Western Osprey
*Pandion haliaetus*

Honey-buzzard, European Honey Buzzard
*Pernis apivorus*

Sparrowhawk, Eurasian Sparrowhawk
*Accipiter nisus*

Goshawk, Northern Goshawk
*Accipiter gentilis*

Marsh Harrier, Western Marsh Harrier
*Circus aeruginosus*

Hen Harrier
*Circus cyaneus*

Red Kite
*Milvus milvus*

Buzzard, Common Buzzard
*Buteo buteo*

Barn Owl, Western Barn Owl
*Tyto alba*

Little Owl
*Athene noctua*

Short-eared Owl
*Asio flammeus*

Tawny Owl
*Strix aluco*

Hoopoe, Eurasian Hoopoe
*Upupa epops*

Kingfisher, Common Kingfisher
*Alcedo atthis*

Wryneck, Eurasian Wryneck
*Jynx torquilla*

Lesser Spotted Woodpecker
*Dryobates minor*

Great Spotted Woodpecker
*Dendrocopos major*

Green Woodpecker, European Green Woodpecker
*Picus viridis*

Kestrel, Common Kestrel
*Falco tinnunculus*

Merlin
*Falco columbarius*

Hobby, Eurasian Hobby
*Falco subbuteo*

Peregrine, Peregrine Falcon
*Falco peregrinus*

Jay, Eurasian Jay
*Garrulus glandarius*

Magpie, Eurasian Magpie
*Pica pica*

Jackdaw, Western Jackdaw
*Coloeus monedula*

Rook
*Corvus frugilegus*

Carrion Crow
*Corvus corone*

Raven, Northern Raven
*Corvus corax*

Coal Tit
*Periparus ater*

Marsh Tit
*Poecile palustris*

Blue Tit, Eurasian Blue Tit
*Cyanistes caeruleus*

Great Tit
*Parus major*

Bearded Tit, Bearded Reedling
*Panurus biarmicus*

Woodlark
*Lullula arborea*

Skylark, Eurasian Skylark
*Alauda arvensis*

Sand Martin
*Riparia riparia*

Swallow, Barn Swallow
*Hirundo rustica*

House Martin, Common House Martin
*Delichon urbicum*

Cetti's Warbler
*Cettia cetti*

Long-tailed Tit
*Aegithalos caudatus*

Wood Warbler
*Phylloscopus sibilatrix*

Yellow-browed Warbler
*Phylloscopus inornatus*

Willow Warbler
*Phylloscopus trochilus*

Chiffchaff, Common Chiffchaff
*Phylloscopus collybita*

Aquatic Warbler
*Acrocephalus paludicola*

Sedge Warbler
*Acrocephalus schoenobaenus*

Reed Warbler, Eurasian Reed
Warbler
*Acrocephalus scirpaceus*

Grasshopper Warbler, Common
Grasshopper Warbler
*Locustella naevia*

Blackcap, Eurasian Blackcap
*Sylvia atricapilla*

Garden Warbler
*Sylvia borin*

Lesser Whitethroat
*Curruca curruca*

Whitethroat, Common Whitethroat
*Curruca communis*

Dartford Warbler
*Curruca undata*

Firecrest, Common Firecrest
*Regulus ignicapilla*

Goldcrest
*Regulus regulus*

Wren, Eurasian Wren
*Troglodytes troglodytes*

Nuthatch, Eurasian Nuthatch
*Sitta europaea*

Treecreeper, Eurasian Treecreeper
*Certhia familiaris*

Rose-coloured Starling, Rosy
Starling
*Pastor roseus*

Starling, Common Starling
*Sturnus vulgaris*

Blackbird, Common Blackbird
*Turdus merula*

Fieldfare
*Turdus pilaris*

Redwing
*Turdus iliacus*

Song Thrush
*Turdus philomelos*

Mistle Thrush
*Turdus viscivorus*

Spotted Flycatcher
*Muscicapa striata*

Robin, European Robin
*Erithacus rubecula*

Nightingale, Common Nightingale
*Luscinia megarhynchos*

Black Redstart
*Phoenicurus ochruros*

Redstart, Common Redstart
*Phoenicurus phoenicurus*

Whinchat
*Saxicola rubetra*

Stonechat, European Stonechat
*Saxicola rubicola*

Wheatear, Northern Wheatear
*Oenanthe oenanthe*

House Sparrow
*Passer domesticus*

Dunnock
*Prunella modularis*

Yellow Wagtail, Western Yellow
Wagtail
*Motacilla flava*

Grey Wagtail
*Motacilla cinerea*

Pied Wagtail
*Motacilla alba yarrelli*

White Wagtail
*Motacilla alba*

Meadow Pipit
*Anthus pratensis*

Tree Pipit
*Anthus trivialis*

Water Pipit
*Anthus spinoletta*

Rock Pipit, European Rock Pipit
*Anthus petrosus*

Chaffinch, Common Chaffinch
*Fringilla coelebs*

Brambling
*Fringilla montifringilla*

Hawfinch
*Coccothraustes coccothraustes*

Bullfinch, Eurasian Bullfinch
*Pyrrhula pyrrhula*

Greenfinch, European Greenfinch
*Chloris chloris*

Linnet, Common Linnet
*Linaria cannabina*

Lesser Redpoll
*Acanthis cabaret*

Goldfinch, European Goldfinch
*Carduelis carduelis*

Siskin, Eurasian Siskin
*Spinus spinus*

Snow Bunting
*Plectrophenax nivalis*

Yellowhammer
*Emberiza citrinella*

Reed Bunting
*Emberiza schoeniclus*

# Appendix 2 - Systematic List of Records *seen prior to 2000 only*

Little Auk
*Alle alle*

Sabine's Gull
*Xema sabini*

Manx Shearwater
*Puffinus puffinus*

Hoopoe, Eurasian Hoopoe
*Upupa epops*